DATE DUE			
~~ILL 14/09~~			
ILL 10/12			

Like It Was

Like It Was

A Complete Guide to Writing Oral History

•

Cynthia Stokes Brown

Teachers & Writers Collaborative
New York, N.Y.

Like It Was: a Complete Guide to Writing Oral History

Cover photo: Rudy Burckhardt, New York, ca. 1939

Teachers & Writers Collaborative
5 Union Square West
New York, N.Y. 10003

Library of Congress Cataloging-in-Publication Data

Brown, Cynthia Stokes.
    Like it was: a complete guide to writing oral history / Cynthia
Stokes Brown.
       p.   cm.
    Bibliography: p.
    Summary: Gives instructions for writing oral histories and
biographies including such aspects as planning, interviewing.,
transcribing, editing, and publishing the results.
    ISBN 0-915924-12-9 (pbk.)
    1. Oral history—Handbooks, manuals, etc.—Juvenile literature.
[1. Oral history—Handbooks, manuals, etc.] I. Title.
D16.14.B76 1988
907'.2—dc19

                                               88-18187

Printed by Philmark Lithographics, New York, N.Y.
Fifth Printing

Table of Contents

Table of Figures

Acknowledgments

Thanks to Herb Kohl, who set this book in motion, told me about his experiences teaching oral history, and encouraged me from beginning to end.

Thanks to Nancy van Ravenswaay, colleague in Global Education Marin and the North Bay International Studies Project, who suggested several of the activities in chapter 9, and to Leslie Marks and Beverly Ludwig, for their work with Grandmother Stories.

Thanks to Jennifer Kaufman, now a sophomore at Berkeley High School, who talked to me about her assignments in oral history.

Thanks to my students—Carol Burns, Jerry Mackay, and Gail Stoltz—for their fifth–grade curriculum unit on the R.M.S. *Titanic*, which gave me the idea for the *Titanic* as a metaphor for how history has been written.

—C.S.B.

Teachers & Writers Collaborative receives funds from the New York State Council on the Arts and the National Endowment for the Arts.

T&W programs and publications are also made possible by funding from the American Broadcasting Companies, Inc., American Stock Exchange, Columbia Committee for Community Service, Consolidated Edison Company, Fund for Poetry, Herman Goldman Foundation, KIDS Fund, Long Island Community Foundation, Mobil Foundation, Inc., Morgan Guaranty Trust Company, Morgan Stanley, New York Telephone, The New York Times Company Foundation, Henry Nias Foundation, Pisces Foundation, Primerica Foundation, Helena Rubinstein Foundation, and The Scherman Foundation.

T&W extends special gratitude to Mr. Bingham's Trust for Charity for its extraordinary commitment to fostering writing and creative thinking skills in children.

Gratitude is also due to the following publishers and writers who permitted T&W to use selections from their work:

Revision advice reproduced, by permission of the publisher, from *Transcribing and Editing Oral History* by Willa K. Baum, Nashville: American Association for State and Local History, 1977, 1981, 1985, 1987.

Excerpt from interview with the Shah of Iran from *Interviews with History* by Oriana Fallaci, Liveright Publishing Corporation, © 1976. Reprinted by permission of the publisher.

Two letters to parents by Bev Ludwig, reprinted by permission of the author.

Radical Elders questionnaire from the Radical Elders Oral History Project (now merged with the Meiklejohn Civil Liberties Institute), whose archives are now in the Meikeljohn Collection. Reprinted by permission of the Meikeljohn Civil Liberties Institute.

Excerpts from *You and Aunt Arie* by Pamela Wood, IDEAS, Inc., 1975, reprinted by permission of the publisher.

Introduction

This book is about writing the stories of people's lives from tape recordings. It tells how to use a tape recorder, how to conduct interviews, and how to write up those interviews as family documents, short articles, or books.

This is written for secondary school and college students who want to write oral histories and for teachers who want to teach them how. Anyone twelve years old or so can pick up this book and get started. If you have a friend, relative, or colleague who is also interested, you can use this book together. If you are a young person who wants to write an oral history, you may be able to persuade a teacher to introduce these skills in the classroom.

If you are a teacher who would like to teach these skills to your students, you may want to practice first by conducting an interview and writing it up yourself. Or you can just start the classroom activities and learn along with your students.

Although this book can be used on its own, it can be used even better as a companion to an oral history called *Ready from Within: Septima Clark and the Civil Rights Movement* (Wild Trees Press, 1986), which I compiled. Septima Clark was a black teacher and grassroots civil rights leader; her narrative provides readers with an introduction to the civil rights movement from a black feminist perspective. When *Ready from Within* is read along with this book, it provides a model of how the transcription of oral interviews can be shaped into literary forms. An instruction manual is rarely sufficient for students of writing; they also need texts that inspire them and demonstrate the skills they wish to obtain.

Students and teachers seldom write history; they usually read it. But that is changing as the understanding spreads that writing must be undertaken across the curriculum. Writing is so basic that it needs to be practiced and enjoyed in every discipline. English teachers may teach the technical and mechanical aspects of writing, but to develop real fluency and power, students need opportunities to apply their writing skills across disciplinary boundaries. This book describes in detail challenging and interesting ways that young people can actually write history.

Writing oral history is not brand new to American schools; it is simply coming around again in the guise of "writing across the curriculum." The last time around it was called "cultural journalism."

The best known project in cultural journalism took place at Rabun Gap High School in the Appalachian Mountains in northern Georgia. Students there began publishing their material locally in 1967 in a little magazine called *Foxfire*, the name of a local organism that glows in the dark. In 1972 the first book of Foxfire articles was published nationally; called *The Foxfire Book*, it became a bestseller and has sold more than two million copies.

Since then nine more Foxfire compilations have been published. A board has been set up to administer the money earned from these sales; most of it has gone into buying land and setting up model villages that preserve the artifacts of a vanishing way of life. Students at Rabun Gap High School are still producing *Foxfire* under the guidance of their teacher, Eliot Wigginton.

The Foxfire project stands for the idea that high school students, not just adults and outsiders, should take part in documenting the cultural life of their community. So much rich ore, fast disappearing, was to be mined that the task required all helpers available. And no better passage into adulthood could be imagined than having young people document the values of their community's wise elders.

During the 1970s many projects similar to Foxfire grew up around the country, in a variety of communities. They became important ways for submerged ethnic minorities to document and celebrate their cultures and to build their own power base from which to deal with the dominant culture.

Some of these projects were:

Bittersweet	Lebanon, Missouri
Salt	Kennebunk, Maine
Nanih Waiya	Philadelphia, Mississippi (native American)
Kil-Kaas-Git	Craig, Alaska
Adobe	San Luis, Colorado
Sea Chest	Cape Hatteras, North Carolina
Tsa'Aszi'	Ramah, New Mexico (Navaho)

Shipjack	Maryland
Peenie Wallie	Jamaica
Cityscape	Washington, D.C.
Streetlight	Chicago
Kalikaq	Bethel, Alaska
Kwikpugmuit	Emmonak, Alaska
Laulima	Honaka, Hawaii
Mo 'olelo	Kaumakani, Hawaii
Golden Hindesight	San Anselmo, California

Two of these also published books that received national distribution: *The Salt Book* (Doubleday, 1977) and *Bittersweet County* (Doubleday, 1978). By the late '70s there were at least 145 cultural journalism publications appearing in the United States.

But oral history was not a popular activity in schools much before Foxfire for the simple reason that it is difficult to accomplish without cheap, portable, effective tape recorders. The first professional portable tape recorder in the United States appeared in 1950. By the late '60s tape recorders had become widely accessible and had helped to transform the very nature of how we think about history.

In non-literate societies, the oral tradition is revered because it is the way that people keep their history alive. In western Africa, for example, certain tribes had their own trained historians called "griots" who stored the history of the entire community in the their memories. The older griots trained young people to take their places, so that the history of the tribe could be passed down indefinitely.

In southeastern Africa, in the Transkei area of South Africa, there lives a woman named Nongenile Masithathu Zenani who, in the '70s, performed an oral narrative that took her seventeen days and 150 hours to complete. It consisted of a fictional tale, filled with historical and ethnographic data, of at least forty story designs that she shaped into a unified whole.

But in the Western tradition, oral historians have been superceded by accounts written for the tiny elite group that could read and write. In this tradition, history has been conceived of as the story of kings (and a few queens) fighting wars. Periods of peace were seen as resting times between wars when nothing much happened. The masses of people were not really considered part of history; it was something that happened *to* them, something that kings and their advisors decided and God ordained. Usually God's representatives, the priests, were allied with the kings. Religious differences provided the rationale for many wars.

This view of history prevailed partly because the writers of history had to depend on very limited sources. Only kings and priests and their close associates had the time, wealth, and skills to record their activities and point of view. Paper and education were not easily available. Writing diaries on sheepskin was difficult and expensive, too; very few could do it.

As time passed, more people had access to paper and quills and to the education necessary to learn to write. The key invention, of course, was the printing press, which after the mid-fifteenth century made possible the creation of multiple copies of memoirs, accounts, and ideas. As more accounts became available, history was expanded to include stories about more people—politicians, philosophers, poets, explorers, scientists.

The nineteenth century saw a furious production of new history; libraries were established to collect archives, and universities grew around them to support historian/scholars in their activity. Trained historians, usually from upper class backgrounds, put together narratives based on the printed and archival sources available to them.

The history produced in the nineteenth century and the twentieth, up to World War II, is now seen as having been centered on political history. It focused on national politics, political and constitutional ideas, and the men who figured in these arenas.

But the vast majority of people did not appear in these history books. For example, the glories of Greece were described with no mention that for every free male citizen in Greece there were at least seven slaves. What was life like for Greek slaves? We do not have testimony from them.

Advances in medicine were chronicled with no mention that when hospitals first began, thousands of women died of childbed fever, spread by the contaminated hands of male physicians. Only men's experiences were considered worthy to be part of the record.

A metaphor for this type of history can be found in the luxury ship, the *Titanic*. When it sailed on its maiden voyage in 1912, its first–class passengers paid the equivalent of $55,000 for their passage across the Atlantic. On board were 2,206 passengers and crew; when the ship hit an iceberg and sank, 703 people were rescued. Those rescued included sixty-three percent of the first-class passengers, forty-two percent of the second class, twenty-five percent of the third class, and twenty-three percent of the crew. Diaries that describe the experience of the first–class passengers on the top deck survived along with them; nothing tells us what it was like on the lower decks. The *Titanic* can serve as a metaphor for what history has been—a view from the top deck, with the elite speaking for the rest, except in rare instances.

But since World War II, history has been opened to everyone. Voices are now being heard that were never heard before—the voices of workers, prisoners, slaves, immigrants, suppressed minorities, and children and young people. History is now "herstory," as well.

Every human event can be seen from different points of view, and every point of view is true in its limited way. Consider what goes on in a family of four. All four members will describe differently what is happening or has happened, and all are accurate. Only someone who can analyze and assimilate all the separate accounts can arrive at an understanding that encompasses the whole. Rarely, this may be one or more members of the family; usually it is an outsider.

In writing history, we can never write a completely accurate account, because the complexity we face is too immense. We make certain assumptions that we are not aware of, and then we have to revise our story when we come up against new evidence that does not fit what we expected.

A good example of that is provided by our attempts to understand the French Revolution. U.S. historians (male) had usually described the French Revolution as being created by men; no women were mentioned. The primary sources for these accounts were the arrest records in Paris; they listed only men who had been arrested for demonstrating.

Eventually female researchers looked beyond the arrest records into eye-witness accounts of the bread strikes in Paris. These eye-witnesses wrote that women led the bread strikes—almost always a woman with a babe at her breast. Now historians hypothesize that women leaders borrowed a baby, if necessary, to foil the police, who certainly wouldn't arrest a nursing mother.

Now that we have tape recorders to record more eye-witness accounts, we will have more sources to work from. Oral history projects at universities and in communities are busy taping the stories of as many people as possible in order for their accounts to serve as primary sources for historians of the future. Writing history on a large scale has become even more difficult than previously, because many more points of view must be taken into account. But becoming clearer about what really happened in the past puts everyone in closer touch with reality and helps us all realize that each person is an actor with the power to affect the script.

The tape recorder is playing a major role in this transformation. It gives voice to people without the time, resources, or skill to write detailed accounts of their experience, people who are, however, skilled at telling their story orally. In order to be heard widely and to be preserved, these storytellers need the assistance of writers who can transcribe their stories into literary forms, and that is where you come in.

Now that tape recorders are relatively cheap and accessible to most people, you too can write history from oral interviews. Why would you want to do that? Here are some reasons:

• You would be helping to put the people into history who belong there. You would be learning the history that is not available anywhere else or any other way.

• You would be serving the people you chose to interview and record.

• You would be explaining and celebrating your community's values, presenting its history as seen from the inside. Outsiders writing about your community are bound to value and describe things differently than your narrators would.

• You would be learning about the moral decisions that people have to make. An interview constitutes a way for you to talk with your elders about issues of great importance, which otherwise might not be discussed and which you need to be aware of as you make your choices.

• You would be meeting special, wonderful people with whom you might form a deep human bond.

• You would be honing your skills as a writer, which will enable you as an adult to play a more powerful role in creating the history of your community and world.

This book will help you. Since there is no substitute for doing yourself what you want to learn, the first chapters move you right into getting a tape recorder, choosing a person to interview, and conducting the interviews. If you already have experience writing from transcriptions, or if you are a teacher who wants to learn along with your students, you may want to start with chapter 9, "How to Do Oral History in the Classrooms." If you need more inspiration to get started, read some oral histories. You might start with *Ready from Within* and then read chapter 1, "Looking Closely at *Ready from*

Within." You can find descriptions of additional oral histories in chapter 10. Good luck!

•

Note: At certain points in this book, I've had to use "he" when referring to a non-specific person. But I want it to be clear that oral history is for everybody, female and male, as interviewers, narrators, and readers.

Looking Closely at
Ready from Within

A good way to get started with writing oral biography is to read some of it. You can avoid lots of blind alleys if you watch how other writers go about it and if you imitate their solutions. But maybe you would rather get started working on one rather than reading some-one else's. If so, skip this chapter and go on to the next one.

Even if you start by interviewing, eventually you will want to read oral biography to develop your awareness of the problems of the genre and how to overcome them. Also, of course, you will want to read to take pleasure in the art of those who have learned to craft fine oral biography and history. This chapter suggests some ways to think about the oral biographies you read.

At the end of this book you will find a list of excellent oral biographies and histories that you can read for pleasure and instruction. I have organized the list into a kind of map of the different kinds of writing that can be done on the basis of oral interviews and have added my comments about each one. You may want to look over that list before proceeding.

But you have to begin reading somewhere, so why not start with *Ready from Within?* It is easy to read and includes some interesting history of the civil rights movement. It seems simple but actually is quite complex and will reward your close examination.

You will enjoy *Ready from Within* most if you can find people who will read it with you. This group might be your family, or a group of friends, or a literary club that you convene to meet regularly and discuss books. It might be a literary club at school — or a whole classroom in English, history, or social studies. Two teachers might be persuaded to use this book in an unified curriculum in history and English.

Before Reading *Ready from Within*

It makes sense to talk about a book before you read it. All of us get impressions and ideas about a book as we decide whether or not to read it. It helps us think if we talk about these ideas with friends or classmates. If you are in class, you could talk together in pairs before the whole class discusses these ideas; that way everybody gets to talk.

Here is a set of questions to discuss before reading *Ready from Within*. Some of these questions have no specific answer; they will stir up speculation about the book. Others have specific answers that can be found by examination of the copyright page, the acknowledgements, the note about the editor, the table of contents, and the note on sources. These sections of a book provide clues that are helpful to read before launching into the main body of any book.

Before Questions
• Examine the book. Guess what is in it. What do you expect to find in it? What's in it for you?
• Study the pictures of Mrs. Clark on the front and back. What kind of a person does she seem to be? Why might a book be written about her? Why would someone decide to use different pictures of her on the front and back? How old was she in both photos? (See page 23, the copyright page, and the caption on the back cover.)
• What do you suppose the title means? What does it mean to you? Do you think it is an effective way to get people's attention? As you read, see if you can find clues to what the title means to Mrs. Clark and why it might have been chosen.
• Is this book history or fiction? What clues can you find by examining the note on the editor, the copyright, and the note on sources.
• Who wrote the book—Mrs. Clark or Cynthia Brown? What kind of a person is the editor? Why might she want to put so much work into creating this particular book?
• Who is the publisher of this book? What kind of a publisher might want to publish a book like this one?

Now for some questions to discuss during or after reading *Ready from Within*. Naturally, the best questions come from you yourself, as you read. You will probably want to talk about Mrs. Clark and what the book says about the civil rights movement— that is, the content of the book.

9

When you have finished this discussion, you can look at the literary qualities of the book. Go over the "Before Questions" again; you will have revised or confirmed your initial guesses and will want to talk about them.

Now for some questions to think about after reading.

After Questions

• What do you think the book's main idea is? Naturally, Septima Clark may think it is one idea, I may think another, and you a third. But amazing as it seems, most books have a single core idea. For me, the core idea of *Ready from Within* is that social movements are created by many people working together, men and women, blacks and whites. What other statements of a possible core idea can you and your friends formulate? You may want to write down your main ideas; doing so helps you think more clearly.

• What level of language is used in this book? Is it dialect or not? Find some specific examples. Would another level of language have been more effective?

• What is Mrs. Clark's perspective or point of view?

• How did the editor find out about Mrs. Clark other than by interviewing her? (See note on sources.) How did the editor add background material that was needed but was missing in Mrs. Clark's account?

• What did the interviewer do with herself in the book? What is the function of the introduction? Does it fulfill its function? What other choices did the interviewer have about dealing with her role in the book?

When you and your friends have finished discussing *Ready from Within*, each of you can write a review of the book in order to have a record of what you really think about it. Maybe you can post some of your reviews in bookstores or in libraries; maybe you can get them published in school, church, club, or town newspapers.

You might want to compare your reviews with some of the published ones. Your reviews probably dealt with more aspects of the book than did the published reviews. These reviewers tended to focus on Mrs. Clark's life, using their reviews to bring recognition to her achievements. But they did not usually analyze the book as a literary document. See figures 1, 2, and 3 for samples of the reviews that have appeared.

An Invaluable Document On Civil Rights Movement

Ready From Within
By Septima Clark
and Cynthia Stokes Brown
Wild Trees Press, P.O. Box 378, Navarro
CA 95463; 134 pages; $8.95

The presence of Martin Luther King looms as an inspiring yet contradictory figure in this quietly astonishing book by one of the Civil Rights Movement's most valuable leaders, Septima Clark.

In her 80s when she taped this oral history for Berkeley writer Cynthia Brown, Clark recalls with profound simplicity how she built a network of "Citizenship Schools" across the South from 1955 to 1970 that resulted in the registration of nearly 2 million black people.

Clark, it appears, has seen it all: black people killed at "nonviolent" marches; black churches bursting into flame; military tanks set up to intimidate black people from registering (they prayed in front of the tanks as they walked by); children killed protecting their mothers from police; toilets above her jail cell that were made to flush "all the stuff" into her room; nurses who refused to soil themselves by pushing shirt sleeves up the arms of black children; black preachers who turned against her because, she knew, "they were dependent on white peoples' approval."

Yet for all this, Clark's story is so undramatically told that we move behind the violence to see how ordinary black people "conspired" to shape the huge registration drives in the South.

At the time, Clark points out, a black person could not register to vote without passing a literacy test that many blacks felt was reprehensible.

In Alabama, one of the questions was: "Give the definition of a thief." The answer: "A thief is a nigger who steals." "In Louisiana," Clark writes, "even the women had to say, 'I am not the father of an illegitimate child.' "

The means by which Clark got around such barriers were both practical and humorous. At one bank in Tuskegee, she says, the registrar hid in a vault whenever he saw a black person coming. One day a very fair-skinned black woman walked in. "When the man came out to register her, the other black people surged in. He said, 'Oh, my God. Here come the niggers.' They thought they had a white woman, but she was one of us."

Clark says she never could have stood up to any white person if it hadn't been for her shouting matches with Myles Horton, founder of Highlander Folk School, the first fully integrated school and farm in the deep South.

Horton "thought I could go right into (a black) community and get a large group of people, talk to them and then ... get them registered." But Clark pressed her "newfangled ideas" that literacy teachers should first listen to the needs of their students, then construct reading lessons to fit those needs.

In Georgia, for example, a common problem was voiced when one woman said she had to ask white people to make out her checks. "So we started teaching banking. We brought in a banker, and he put the whole form up on the board .. " Even after the banker was driven out of town by angry farmers, says Clark, black people were finally able to withdraw their own money from the banks.

She regards her tenure as the only female member of the executive board of the Southern Chris-

Septima Clark: A new voice for the movement

tian Leadership Conference as a mixed blessing. "Those men didn't have any faith in women," she writes. "That's why Rev. Abernathy would say continuously, "Why is Mrs. Clark on this staff?' ... I had a great feeling that Dr. King didn't think much of women either. He would laugh and say, "Ha, ha, ha. Mrs. Clark has expanded our program.' That's all."

King is seen here as making his followers feel that "you can work behind the scenes all you want ... but don't come forth and try to lead." This is the only note of bitterness in Septima Clark's invaluable document, and strangely enough, it is a welcome one. Before King becomes a complete legend, such "new" voices as that of Septima Clark remind us that there were many strong and visionary leaders behind the Civil Rights Movement in the South.

Figure 1: Review from the *San Francisco Chronicle*

Septima Poinsette Clark's story, as recorded by historian Cynthia Stokes Brown, gives a deeper perspective to Robinson's and King's, for she is an authentic pioneer in Southern militancy. Clark, who as a young woman worked in the, desperately poor island schools on the South Carolina coast, honed her organizing skills at the famous Highlander Folk School in Tennessee. It was there she found in herself the power, as she puts it, "to speak my mind to a white man." In 1956, she was dismissed from her post as a Charleston, South Carolina, teacher for refusing to renounce membership in the NAACP. Throughout her 60s and 70s, she trained community organizers, including the redoubtable Fannie Lou Hamer, and on her 79th birthday Mrs. Clark gained sweet vindication by becoming the first black woman elected to the Charleston School Board.

These memoirs all demonstrate the pride that. comes with finding one's political voice and the satisfaction of knowing that one has served the cause of justice. For all of SNCC's deficiencies and mistakes, Mary King writes, "I still feel I was part of something so extraordinary that it almost defies description." And Septima Clark, whose mother paid for a few years of schooling by washing and ironing long past midnight, describes the changes of her lifetime by saying simply, "The air has finally gotten to the place that we can breathe it together."

READY FROM WITHIN: Septima Clark and the Civil Rights Movement *Edited and with an introduction by Cynthia Stokes Brown.* Wild Trees Press (P.O. Box 378, Navarro, Calif. 95463), $8.95 ISBN 0-931125-04-9

In 1979, Brown spent a week interviewing Clark, who was then 81 and had spent a good part of her life struggling for civil rights in South Carolina. Brown subsequently edited and rearranged Clark's story, which is variously told in standard English, an African-inspired version spoken on St. John's Island, S.C., and Charlestonese. The result is a rich tale—Clark was a teacher for years, until she was fired in 1956 because of her membership in the NAACP. Soon she became involved in the Citizenship Schools, which trained black adults to read and write in order to be eligible to vote. Later she worked with Martin Luther King Jr., Rosa Parks and others in the Southern Christian Leadership Conference. Today near 90, Clark carries on her struggle, working with black women, who as a group, she maintains, have to face greater obstacles than most other people. This is a poignant story, told with hope and humanity.

Ready from Within: Septima Clark and the Civil Rights Movement, edited with an introduction by Cynthia Stokes Brown (Wild Trees Press, $8.95). This short oral history, based on a series of interviews conducted with teacher and organizer Septima Poinsette Clark, is more a sampling of her varied life than a complete and comprehensive presentation of it. The daughter of a former slave and cook who became a successful caterer, Clark was training director of the Voter Education Project. A textured portrait of a spunky and inspiring woman.

Figure 2: Reviews from *New York Newsday, Publishers Weekly,* and *Ms.*

An early civil rights pioneer

New book reveals magnitude of Septima Clark's role

By Barbara L. Sloane
Special to The Voice

Ready From Within: Septima Clark and the Civil Rights Movement, by Septima Clark, edited by Cynthia Stokes Brown; published by Wild Trees Press.

The name Septima Clark is not one quickly recognized by Americans remembering the early days of the civil rights movement. Even Cynthia Stokes Brown of Berkeley, the editor of Clark's biography, admits to her initial ignorance of this woman's important role in the movement.

Born in 1898 in Charleston, South Carolina, Septima Clark became a public school teacher as a young woman. However, in 1956 she was fired because she would not resign her membership in the National Association for the Advancement of Colored People. Subsequently, working through the Highlander Folk School in Tennessee, she toured the southern states, setting up "citizenship schools" to teach black adults basic literacy in preparation for voting.

Ready From Within: Septima Clark and the Civil Rights Movement recounts the magnitude of the task facing Clark, and her amazing victory. Brown writes:

"In 1955 only about 25 percent of voting-age blacks were registered in the 11 Deep South states. More than 3.5 million weren't registered, and many of them couldn't read. Working with others, Clark figured out how to teach them to read in two or three months' time. By 1970 nearly 2 million more black people were voting than had been in 1955."

Clark's work in the 1960s brought her into close contact with Dr. Martin Luther King, Jr., Rosa Parks, Andrew Young of the Southern Christian Leadership Conference and other well-known figures of the civil rights movement. Today Clark lives in Charlestown, where she served as the first black woman on the school board from 1978 to 1983.

Those are the facts of Septima Clark's life, little-known to the general public. However, Cynthia Brown's book is changing all that. Published in November by Wild Trees Press, this first-person narrative, edited by Brown, brings the vital educator Clark to life for a reader.

The soft-spoken Brown retains a touch of her own Southern roots in her speech. Educated at Duke University and Johns Hopkins University, she began her teaching career in history in Baltimore. Following two years as the wife of a Peace Corps physician in Brazil, she settled in Berkeley, where she lives today.

An associate professor of education at Dominican College in San Rafael, Brown trains future elementary and secondary teachers. She has published two earlier books, *Literacy in Thirty Hours: Paulo Freire's Process in Northeast Brasil*, and *Alexander Meiklejohn: Teacher of Freedom*.

Brown's interest in history, literacy and educators makes her a natural choice to tell the story of Septima Clark's achievements. However, Brown, who grew up in Kentucky, acknowledges that she had never heard of the Highlander Folk School in neighboring Tennessee or of Septima Clark until the mid-1970s.

It was then that her friend, Herbert Kohl, met Clark on a visit to the remarkable school where whites and blacks build meet together to discuss problems and attempt to solve them. Upon his return, Kohl urged Cynthia to write Clark's story.

Brown smiles shyly as she says, "He said that Septima's story had to be told by a woman, by a Southener, and by an historian. I fit all the qualifications."

Brown set out for Charleston in 1979 to get some background.

"My original plan was to write this story for teenagers, because so few of them know of any leaders of the movement other than Dr. King," Brown said. "That is one reason there is so much focus on Septima's childhood in the book."

The story, which emerged in Clark's own words, is a moving one of the daughter of a slave who led thousands of her people to real freedom through literacy.

Ready From Within is the first biography published by Wild Trees Press. On March 7, the 89-year-old Clark was present at a reception and book-signing held at the Oakland Museum, sponsored by the press and by the Alpha Kappa Alpha and Delta Sigma Theta sororities. Book selections were read by Angela Davis, Alice Walker, Joyce Carol Thomas and Luisah Teish.

Cynthia Brown has succeeded in presenting Septima Clark's story in Clark's own voice. Speaking forthrightly in *Ready From Within*, Clark herself stresses the essential part she played in the movement when she says, "One time I heard Andy Young say that the citizenship schools were the base on which the whole civil rights movement was built. And that's probably very much true."

Ready From Within *is available for $8.95 from local bookstores or by mail order from Wild Trees Press, P.O. Box 378, Novarro, CA 95463.*

Figure 3: Review from *The Montclarion* (Montclair, CA)

Activities for Practicing Oral History

Playing with Time Lines

Time has a way of getting away from us, even from day to day. Imagine how difficult it is to keep track of time from year to year, or over several decades. In order to visualize time, historians use a simple tool—time lines, which lay out, in a straight line, events that in our heads swim around all muddled up.

• Here is how to make a time line:

1. Find a long sheet of paper, like a roll of white shelf paper. Or tape two or three pieces of typing paper together in a line.

2. Draw a horizontal line across the paper in about the middle.

3. Divide the line with a mark for each year of your life. Make each mark the same distance apart—an inch, or maybe two or three if you want to add decorations or illustrations.

4. Label each mark with the year and your age in that year.

5. Now think about the outstanding, significant events of your life and write them in at the appropriate mark. Everyone has a different idea of what is outstanding and significant. See what the first things you remember are. Find friends who want to make a time line of their lives and compare them when you have each finished your own. You may keep adding events as you talk with parents and friends and recall forgotten events. Using this simplest tool will help you learn to think about time, so that eventually you will be able to do it in your head without using a time line.

Now start a new time line on a longer sheet of paper. Portray the life of someone older—one of your parents would be a good choice. Mark off each year and label with the number of the year. Put down everything you know about your parent's life—what year he or she was born, married, had children, went to war, took a trip, changed jobs, got sick, whatever.

Now get your parent in on this game. You may want to conduct an informal interview, either taking notes or tape-recording. What questions to ask? For starters, how about:

What are the most significant events of your life? When did each occur? What is your earliest memory?

You can transfer the information directly onto your time line as your parent tells it to you, or you can do it later.

If you enjoy this, interview other members of your family and soon you will have a family time line. Do this in early December just for the preceeding year; include every member of the family, and you will have a terrific gift to send to relatives and friends at the holiday season.

• Now arrange a longer sheet of paper—about nine feet. Draw a horizontal line through the middle and mark it off in intervals of five inches. Label each mark for the decades: 1980, 1970, 1960, back to 1780. Make little marks within each decade at half–inch intervals; these mark each year.

Now locate and label three dates: when you, your father or mother, and your grandfather or grandmother were born. When you do this, you are beginning to think in generations. How old were your parents when you were born? How old were your grandparents when your parents were born? What is the average span of a generation in your recent family? (To find it, add the answers of the two previous questions and divide by two.)

A generation is usually considered twenty or twenty-five years. Use twenty-five years as a generation and mark off your time line back to the American Revolution (1776) to see how many generations from it you are. You might want to label each generation with the name of that relative's relationship to you, i.e., great-grandparent (for the mark prior to your grandparent's birthdate), great-great-grandparents, and so on back. What generation of your family came to this country?

Thinking in generations back so far probably seems difficult to you, even with the help of a time line. People in literate cultures are not used to keeping generations in their heads. But non-literate people are; it is the only way their history survives. Listen to this thirteen-year-old black girl in Mississippi tell about her family; she is still living in a tradition brought over from an African society:

My family history goes—well, as far as I know, it goes all the way back to 1700. 1700: Sarah Martha Blakeman was born. She wasn't a slave then. 1731: She was thirty years old; she was captured for a slave. She'd already given birth to Sarah Marie Blakeman. That's my great-great-great-grandmother. Sara Marie Blakeman then gave birth to my great-great-grandmother, Martha Blakeman, who was a part of the Freedom Train [Underground Railroad]. Then *she* gave birth to my great-grandmother, who just died lately, Sarah Marie Blakeman II; and my great-grandmother just told me the story. And my uncle and my great-great-grandmother took part in the Freedom Train. They escaped, but he got scared, and he turned back, but he was killed. My great-great-grandmother

15

walked across the bridge of freedom. I've forgot what year that was in. And not long ago, my great-grandmother died. She was ninety-two. . . . [The information] was passed down the generations. Each time someone was born, about the time they got about twelve, they [were] told. And I'm supposed to pass it on through a generation when I get older. . . . The daughter passes the word down.*

Now add to your time line of generations the date of the birth of Septima Clark. Add several more dates from her life and the main events of the civil rights movement. Look at the chronology (pp. 128–9) in *Ready from Within* for suggestions.

Now you are ready to relate your family's story to the story of the civil rights movement. How old were your grandparents when Mrs. Clark was fired from her teaching job in Charleston in 1956? When the Voting Rights Act was passed in 1965? When Dr. King was assassinated? How old were your parents during these events? What do they remember about them? How did they feel about the civil rights movement and about specific events that occurred? Did they participate in any way? It is time to interview them again and find out.

You may already have a mental framework that organizes time by wars. History is often taught as being one war after another.

• Make a time line that shows your family's relationship to World War II (1939–45), the Korean War (1950–53), and the Vietnam War (1964–75). Once you have constructed a time line of these wars, it will suggest many questions for you to ask your grandparents and parents.

• Make a time line of Mrs. Clark's life. Use the chronology at the back of the book and/or the story itself. Mark her life off into its main periods. When were the decisive moments of her life?

Notice that the story in *Ready from Within* does not start at the beginning of her life and go to the end. How would the story be if it were told this way? Why do you suppose that it starts in 1947 instead of at the beginning of her life? Make a list of the story as it is arranged. It starts in 1947, goes to the 1960s, then where? Is this an effective sequence? Why or why not?

Think about another place in Mrs. Clark's life where the story might have started—some decisive or dramatic moment that would

*A tape recorded interview made in Bentonia, Mississippi, January 28, 1980, Barbara Allen and Lynwood Montell, *From Memory to History: Using Oral Sources in Local Historical Research* (Nashville, Tennessee: American Association for State and Local History, 1981), p. 70.

attract the reader's attention. Pretend that you are editing the transcripts of her story and write the first few paragraphs to start the story at this different place that you have chosen. Use the text as it is —just write whatever sentences you need to get the story started in a different place.

Playing with Voice

• Pretend you have a chance to interview Septima Clark. What questions would you want to ask her? Write them down. Now pretend that you are Mrs. Clark, and ask a friend to interview you, using your questions and any others your friend might want to add. Can you imitate Mrs. Clark's language? Tape this interview, transcribe it, and compare your language to Mrs. Clark's.

• Oral biographies and histories are usually written in the first person voice. The person tells the story in his or her own voice: "I was born in. . . . I did thus and so. . . ." This constitutes much of the charm and interest of oral biography; the words on the page actually sound like the real person telling the story.

But there are problems with a first-person narrative. For example, the person telling the story may leave out some information that the reader needs in order to understand the story. The narrator often assumes the readers know more than they do. For example, when Mrs. Clark talked about the NAACP, she didn't explain what the NAACP is; she assumed everyone would know that it stood for the National Association for the Advancement of Colored People. But, of course, many people, especially young people, do not know about the NAACP. What to do?

For a while, I thought that I would solve the problem of not enough background material by telling the story in the third person ("she was born. . . . She did thus and so. . . .")

By using this device I could add whatever I wanted to, because I had become the narrator. Here are the opening paragraphs of my draft in the third person, showing how I put in background information about Charleston and the NAACP.

> The school term was drawing to a close. As Mrs. Clark got off the bus at her corner, she could distinguish between the warm scent of the first oleander flowers, the exhaust of the bus, and the ever-present odor of the salt of the sea. The beauty of the late May afternoon and the approaching end of school should have filled her with a sense of contentment.
>
> But they did not. She was expecting at any moment to be dis-

missed from her teaching job. The third of June, fast approaching, was the deadline by which the superintendent had to send out a letter to any teacher who would not be re-hired for the fall term. Mrs. Clark knew that she was likely to receive such a letter any day now. She had gotten plenty of clues that her community thought she was going a little too far in her work to break down the segregation of races in Charleston. . . .

She knew that the school authorities had the legal right to discharge her without giving her any reason for doing so. That reason had nothing to do with her teaching, but with an organization she belonged to. It was called the National Association for the Advancement of Colored People, or NAACP for short.

The NAACP had been formed forty-seven years before — in 1909 — in New York City. Mrs. Clark had joined in 1918, when she was twenty years old and just beginning her work as a teacher. Since it had only cost a dollar a year in membership fees, she had been able to afford membership. Sometimes she had been impatient with how slowly the local chapters of this group had worked to improve conditions for black people, but she had been a member all those years.

Then in 1955 the legislature of South Carolina had passed a law stating that no city or state employee could belong to the NAACP. The legislature had never before made it illegal to belong to the NAACP, but they did so then in reaction to a ruling by the U.S. Supreme Court.

A year earlier, in May 1954, the U.S. Supreme Court had ruled that segregation by race in public schools violated the U.S. Constitution and must be ended. Most white legislators in South Carolina did not agree with the U.S. Supreme court, and there were no black people in the state legislature. The legislators wanted to resist the Supreme Court's ruling any way they could.

One way they tried was to pass a law saying that no city or state employee could belong to the NAACP. They hoped that might frighten members of the NAACP enough so that they would not push for integration of black and whites in the public schools. After the law passed, school administrators gave out questionnaires to teachers, who had to list all the organizations they belonged to. Mrs. Clark refused to overlook her membership in the NAACP; she listed it.

Compare this to the first-person version in *Ready from Within* (pp. 35–36). Which do you prefer? I re-wrote the whole story in the third-person before I convinced myself that I did not like it as

18

much. It seemed to lack authenticity, even if there were more details. I realized I could add details in a note like the one on pp. 39–40.

Try it yourself. Pick a short passage and re-write it in the third person. This sort of practice will give you the command you need as a writer, the skill to choose whatever voice seems most effective to you.

Playing Novelist

• Sometimes a writer decides to create an oral biography, not by interviewing someone, but by making up a story as if it were an interview with a real person. Such a book is *The Autobiography of Miss Jane Pittman* by Ernest Gaines. Are you the sort of person who would find it easier to make up a story than to conduct an interview, transcribe the tapes, and go through all that process? If you can do it in your imagination, more power to you.

Read *Miss Jane Pittman* and compare it to *Ready from Within*. How can you tell that one is fiction and the other is not?

Both of these books are aimed at a young adult audience. This genre is often characterized by a simplification of theme and characterization, i.e., people portrayed not as complexly as they are in real life. Does this seem true of either of these books?

Both of these books provide an overview of the civil rights movement. Which do you prefer and why?

CHAPTER 2

Using a Recorder

Cassette recorders are probably old hat for you. You have probably been using one for years, sending tapes instead of letters to relatives or copying music from the tapes of your friends.

If you have had some experience with a cassette recorder, it won't take any time for you to feel comfortable taping interviews. Any cassette recorder will do the job. Don't feel that you need to buy a special one. Borrow one, read the operating manual carefully, and play around with it to become familiar with how your particular machine works.

The simpler you can keep the technical part of oral interviews, the better: your attention needs to be focused on listening to your narrator and on formulating questions. Current cassette recorders are a great help, because basically, you just shove in a cassette and push the "record" button. That's all there is to it.

How a Recorder Works

But it hasn't always been this simple. The first early magnetic recording device, called the "Telegraphone," was introduced by the Danish physicist, Valdemar Poulsen, in 1898. It received a U.S. patent in 1900. Experimentation continued, culminating in the "Magnetophon," developed by a German electrical company, Allgemeine Elektrizitats Gesellschaft (A.E.G.) and publically demonstrated in August 1935 at the Radio Exhibition in Berlin.

Early tape recorders were devices for transforming sound into electric current, which activated an electro-magnet (the "head"). This head magnetized a coating of iron oxide on a constantly moving ribbon (the "tape"). This magnetic imprint varied as the sound varied; a loud sound made a stronger imprint than a soft one, a high sound imprinted a different pattern than a low one. When the recording was played back, the magnetized tape passed over another magnet, the "playback head." The magnetized tape activated the playback head, creating an electrical current that vibrated a speaker, creating sounds.

Many advances in both materials and electronics were required as magnetic recording became practical. Its first widespread use occurred in Germany during World War II when speeches by Hitler and other Nazi leaders were broadcast at times and places calculated to confuse Allied intelligence. Suddenly Hitler was heard talking in one place when he was supposed to be in another!

Meanwhile, German radio stations were broadcasting symphony concerts all night long, a fact noticed by an American GI working late at night in England. This GI, Jack Mullin, knew that these concerts could not be live night after night, and he set out to find the answer of how the broadcast was accomplished.

In July 1945, after the war had ended in defeat for Germany, Jack Mullin was sent there to look into reports that Germans had used high-frequency energy to jam airplane engines in flight. He found nothing of that sort, but near Frankfurt he found a Magnetophone in a castle used as a radio broadcasting station—the answer to where the beautiful night music had come from.

Mullin took two Magnetophones apart and sent them back home to San Francisco in thirty-five separate pieces, boxed to fit inside Army mailbags. They all arrived safely, and in early 1946 Mullin re-assembled the two machines and demonstrated them. One of the early observers was the singer, Bing Crosby, who resented the regimentation imposed on his life by live broadcasts and was looking for a high-quality means to record his performances.

The commitment to develop the Magnetophone in the U.S. was made by an engineering firm near San Francisco called Ampex. Alexander M. Poniatoff, an electrical engineer born in Russia, formed Ampex in 1944. During the war it produced airborne radar motors and generators for the U.S. Navy.

When Ampex was searching for a new, post-war product, one of its engineers saw Jack Mullin's demonstration of the German magnetophones. In December 1946 Ampex began to try to reproduce an audio tape recorder of professional quality. With $50,000 of backing from Bing Crosby, Ampex delivered the first audio recorder to the American Broadcast Company in April 1948, when it was used for the first time to present a delayed broadcast of the Bing Crosby Show.

By 1950, Ampex had received requests to develop equipment to be used for recording data in industrial, military, and scientific research, which it did. Ampex also continued new developments in audio tape recording, including a duplicator system that made it practical to duplicate master tapes for retail sale of pre-recorded high fidelity tapes and the first portable tape recorder designed for professional use (1950). By 1956 Ampex Corporation could demonstrate the first commercial videotape recorder (VTR). Ampex continued its focus on products for professional use and did not market the first cassette tape recorders; those were introduced by the Philips Company of Eindhoven, Netherlands, in 1963.

Tips on Using a Recorder

• **Power Supply**

You need electricity to run a recorder. This electricity can be supplied by house current (you plug in the recorder) or by batteries (you don't).

The advantage of house current is that it is dependable (it doesn't run down as batteries do) and it is cheaper. The disadvantage is that you have to conduct your interview within an extension cord's reach of an electrical outlet.

Most cassette recorders do not even come with a way to plug them in; they rely entirely on batteries. Others can be plugged in, but you have to buy an accessory called a "power pack". It is worth the price (about $15) because of the cost in batteries it saves.

A good rule to follow: never use batteries for anything but interviewing—and not then if you can conveniently avoid it. Always use house current for playback and transcribing.

Now for batteries. They come in two types and many sizes. They also vary in quality—how much work you can get out of them before they go dead.

Plain old carbon-zinc "flashlight" batteries can be used only one–two hours a day, with a day or two in between to recuperate. They can only give about eight hours of total use, and they cannot be left in the machine more than a week because they are likely to leak. Within these constraints, they are fine.

Alkaline (manganese dioxide) batteries cost about four times as much and last about four times as long. They will work for several hours at a time; they don't need as much time to recuperate; they have less tendency to leak. Unless you cannot affort alkaline batteries, they provide more convenience for the same long-term cost.

Batteries can run down without giving out completely. This may happen without your being aware of it while you are recording. Run-down batteries make the recorder go slower. It records, but does not play back successfully because the tape is not being played back at exactly the same speed at which it was recorded. If you must use batteries to record, remember to check frequently the battery indicator that shows whether the batteries are strong.

• **Tapes**

Tapes come in various sizes. The thinner they are, the more can be gotten on a cassette and the longer they play. But the thinner tapes are more likely to stretch and to print-through (that is, one layer of tape transfers its magnetic imprint to the layer beneath it, giving an echo effect on playback). A good tape for interviews is the thirty-minute tape (C-60). It is the standard thickness, 1.5 mils. The forty-five-minute tape (C-90) can also be used; it's convenient because you don't have to turn it over so often. Never use one-hour tapes (C-120); they are only .5 mil thick and have a good chance of giving problems. Just be sure to get the right size batteries for your machine.

• **The Controls**

On/Off Switch. On most of the inexpensive battery-operated machines, there is no on/off at all; putting the machine in one of its modes (play, record, fast forward, or rewind) turns it on, while taking it out of mode turns it off. Some hand microphones have an on/off switch on their side. This can cause confusion if you plug in the hand mike, put the machine in "record," and nothing happens. If your hand mike has an on/off switch, you will need to turn it on, too.

Play. Pressing this control starts the tape moving; if there is something on the tape, you will hear it. This control may be marked "play," "forward," "fwd," or have an arrow pointing to the right.

Record. Push this button and whatever sounds are going on will be recorded on your tape. If something is already on your tape, it will be erased and covered over with new material. Older recorders had a safety "interlock" feature, whereby the machine would not record unless two buttons were pushed in — "record" and one other, usually "play" but sometimes "pause." With the newer machines you have to be more careful not to leave recorded tape in the machine, because it could be erased if the "record" button were accidentally pressed. Rewind all tapes and remove them at once when you are not listening. To be sure your tapes will *never* be erased, poke in the two plastic "tabs" on the top edge of the cassette.

Pause. This control simply stops the forward motion of the tape without taking the machine out of mode; it stays in "record" or "play." Sometimes the "pause" button has to be held down to be in effect; then releasing it starts the tape again. Sometimes you move it one way to pause, the other way to start up again.

Fast Forward. This mode may be called "advance" or "cue," or it may be marked with double arrows pointing to the right. It moves the tape ahead in a hurry. If you are using batteries, use this mode as little as possible. It wears your batteries down fast, as does "rewind."

Rewind. Sometimes called "reverse" or "review," and sometimes marked with an arrow or a double arrow pointing left, this mode is simply "fast forward backwards." It moves the tape swiftly to the left. If you are using batteries, remember that this mode wears down batteries just as much as "fast forward" does. If you can, wait to rewind your tape until you get to where you can plug in to house current.

Stop. Push this button and your machine stops. Frequently it stops with a loud "click'" to let you know clearly that activity has halted. Always switch from one mode to another by moving through "stop," even if the instructions say this is not necessary. For instance, if you are recording and want to rewind, first push "stop," then "rewind." This saves wear and tear on the switches and prevents excess strain on the tape.

Monitor. This control is usually on one side of the machine, or even on the back. When the monitor is turned on, you can hear what is being recorded played back through the speaker, or through a headset, if you have one plugged in. If you turn the monitor off, the speaker is disconnected while you are in "record." The monitor is not something you use much, if at all, in oral interviewing.

Volume. During recording, most recorders deactivate this control. They use "automatic level control," an internal system that automatically adjusts the recording volume. This is a wonderful convenience, but it has some drawbacks that you should be aware of. First, the "automatic level control" (a.l.c.) cannot be used to record music because it obliterates the loud and soft places in the performance. Second, a.l.c. does not work well in noisy surroundings. It adjusts to the loudest sound available to it. If that happens to be the narrator's voice, then your voice may get lost. Even if your voice isn't lost, the noise around you will swell up to fill any silences that last over a couple of seconds. Remember the a.l.c. is constantly looking for a sound to record, and it doesn't distinguish between a voice and a washing machine. When the voice comes in again, it takes the a.l.c. a split second to adjust again, enough time to lose the first word in an answer. In noisy situations, it is best to record with a machine that has manual volume control and to keep it at as low a level as possible, with a mike kept close to the narrator's mouth.

• **Microphones**

Most tape recorders on the market today have built-in microphones ("mikes"), sometimes called "condenser mikes." These have the advantage of not being noticeable; they reduce stage fright and distraction. Their disadvantage is that they pick up the noise of the recorder's motor and thereby reduce the quality of the narrator's voice on tape. You can try out your machine in various conditions to discover the limits and capabilities of its built-in mike.

Most cassette recorders do not come with an external, or plug-in mike, but for an extra $30 or so, you can purchase one—a worthwhile investment. The external mike plugs into a "jack," a hole usually on the side or front of the recorder. Be careful not to set the microphone on the same surface as the recorder; it will record the reverberations. Keep the mike and the recorder as far apart as possible, so that the mike does not pick up the noise of the motor. If you set the mike on a flat surface, pad it with a folded kleenex, scarf, or glove. If you don't, it may pick up lots of noise moving through the surface of the table, such as the tapping of a pencil or the moving of an ashtray.

Mikes are very sensitive and pick up noise that you won't hear during an interview. You want to place the mike as close as possible to your narrator without bothering or distracting him. The quality of your recording also depends on how low you can keep the volume (or how low the machine can keep the volume, if it is adjusted automatically). The further away the mike is and the higher the volume, the more hollow the voice will be and the more background noise you will get. If you hold the mike right up to the face of your narrator, neither of you will be able to relax much. Try some compromise; try out placements at home and see how they work. If the mike is the "directional" type, you should point it toward your narrator.

• **Cleaning**
Cleaning your tape recorder is necessary for it to function well. This can be done by buying a re-useable cleaning tape for $10–15 that is simply run through the machine every 30–40 hours of recording or playing time.

A much cheaper way to clean your recorder is to buy a bottle of isopropyl (rubbing) alcohol and a box of Q-tips at a drugstore or supermarket. Dip a Q-tip in the alcohol, squeeze it out, and rub it gently over the heads. Don't press too hard or you can scratch the head. You should also clean the tape guide in the same way. The "head" is the shiny metal piece (about $\frac{1}{2}" \times \frac{3}{8}"$) with a rounded front edge, and the "tape guide" consists of a rubber roller and post that hold the tape between them when it's moving. You can see these parts by looking into the slot where the front edge of the tape fits in.

Buying a Recorder

After you have used a borrowed cassette recorder for a while, or an old one that you have inherited from your family, you may want to shop for a new one. Here are some additional features you will need to consider:

Micro or table size? The micro size has the advantage of compactness; it can slip into a pocket or be held and operated in one hand. The larger size produces a better play-back because it has larger speakers and sometimes has a hookup for a foot switch (for ease in transcribing).

Auto reverse: This means that the recorder automatically flips the tape after one side has been recorded. With a C–90 tape, this produces 1½ hours of uninterrupted taping time and eliminates the problem of turning the tape without losing any monologue.

Voice activated: This feature is useful more for dictation than for recording interviews. The tape is activated to record by the voice; it stops whenever there is a pause in the voice.

External microphone: All current models have built-in mikes. They are especially convenient, but seldom get the sound fidelity of an external mike. Most models have jacks for attaching an external mike, which cost from $15 to $5,000(!) for a hand mike and from $35 up for a lapel mike that can be attached to the narrator's shirt or blouse. If you have an external mike, then you can decide in each situation whether the better sound of the remote mike or the unobtrusiveness of the built-in mike is more important.

Foot switch: This allows you to start and stop the playback by foot so that you can type a transcription without lifting your hands from a typewriter. Since a regular business transcribing machine, with foot pedal and earphone, costs around $300, you probably won't have one. You can transcribe without a foot pedal, but it is a helpful option. However, most micro-cassette recorders do not permit this attachment; you must choose between the convenience of a foot pedal on a table model and the convenience of a smaller machine.

End of tape alarm: This goes off near the end of the tape to alert you to the need to change the tape.

Variable speed control: Some recorders can be played back 20% slower than recording speed. This makes transcription easier.

Dual cassettes: This feature allows you to make copies of tapes. You might want to give copies to family members, or to copy rare and valuable tapes and store them in a safe place.

To purchase a recorder, go to the largest store near you and talk with its salespeople about what is available. For a start in making comparisons, here are the specifications for a few models, 1987 prices:

• Sanyo M–1012 (3¼″ × 5½″) $34.95: jack for external mike, jack for power pac.

• Sanyo Slim-8 (5″ × 10″) $34.95: desk model, larger speakers result in better playback quality, includes power pac, jack for external mike, foot switch available @$5.00.

• AIWA TP–27 (3¼″ × 5½″) $119.00: All metal, jack for external mike and power pac (not included); voice activated; auto reverse.

For an excellent catalog of good recording and dictating equipment (nothing under $50), send $2 to Martel Electronics,

Inc., 920–D E. Orangethorpe, Anaheim, CA 92801. This catalog will let you compare the specifications of different brands.

Practice

In order to learn what your recorder and its microphones can do, you can play this game. Set up the tape recorder, put it in record mode, and talk to it, all the time telling it what you are doing at the moment. Keep up a line like this: "Now I have turned this machine on, and I'm talking in a normal voice about two feet from the recorder, which is on the table. Now I've moved back from the machine about four feet and am still talking in a normal voice. Now I've moved to the side and I'm six feet from the machine. Now I have moved the recorder to a noisy room. . . . Now I have plugged in the hand mike and am holding it four feet from my mouth. . . . Now I am operating the volume manually. . . ." Keep up this kind of chatter, exploring as many possibilities as you can think of, describing all the time in detail what you are doing. Play back your tape, study the results, and you will understand how your machine really works.

Practice flipping and changing tapes until this becomes routine. Locate a 30-minute timer to set at 28 minutes to let you know when the end of the tape is approaching; then you can stop your interview before the tape runs out, and nothing will be lost. Use the alarm on your watch, if that is available.

You are now on your way to becoming the master of your machine—cool, confident, collected, able to operate almost on automatic. Now you can turn your attention to the important parts of interviewing—asking questions and listening attentively.

Doing three things at once —operating the machine, asking questions, and listening attentively— constitutes quite a juggling act. To get the hang of it, you might practice doing it with two friends. One can be the narrator, one can be the interviewer, while the third can attend to the machine. Rotate the three roles until each one seems easy to you; then you can combine all of them and manage to keep one eye on the recorder, one on your narrator, and still keep listening and formulating questions all the while.

Setting Out

Before you set out on an interview, make sure you have every piece of equipment you will need. Here is a check list that you can copy and attach to your carrying bag:

- tape recorder
- batteries *or*
    power pac (wall plug) plus extension cord
- tapes plus extra ones
- external mike (optional)
- camera (optional)
- handerchief or kleenex
- timer
- notepad, pencil, questions

Before you leave, check to see that everything is functioning properly. Do this by recording an identification at the beginning of the tape you will use for this interview. On this identification, record the following information: the name of the narrator, the place of the interview, the name of the interviewer (you). Depending on the purpose of your interview, include what you plan to talk about or a brief overview of the life of the narrator.

Here are two samples:

Today is January 4, 1987. We are in San Francisco in the office of Bank of America. We are going to interview the president, Mr. Thomas Clausen, about Mexico's debt and its effect on his bank. The interviewers are Max Green, Susie Armstrong, and Brenda Bay.

This is an interview with Septima Poinsette Clark. Mrs. Clark is the daughter of a slave. She taught in South Carolina from 1916 to 1956, and played a vital role in the civil rights movement by setting up Citizenship Schools from 1957 to 1965. These interviews are being conducted during the week of August 7, 1979, at Mrs. Clark's home on President Street in Charleston. The interviewer is Cynthia Stokes Brown.

•

You will record this identification on the tape *before* arriving for your interview because you want to put your narrator at ease. If you arrive at the interview; begin with this formal announcement, and shove the microphone at your narrator with a gesture of "You're on the air!" you may get total silence. Even listening to this pre-recorded identification may increase your narrator's anxiety, so after you record it, don't rewind the tape. Just leave it in place at the end of the indentification and begin there with your interview. You can also leave enough blank space on the tape for the identification and record it after you have recorded the interview. Either way, be sure the narrator will not be bothered by the formal identification on the tape.

Your final check will also include packing extras of everything you expect to use. Pack extra tapes; your narrator may want to go on much longer than you expect. A tape may tangle and break — rare but possible. Take extra batteries; you never know when batteries will give out.

Your own attitude toward your machine will be conveyed to your narrator. If you are at ease, you will communicate that. If you are not, then try to convey an attitude of playful experimentation, and your narrator will catch that, too. After all, you are not broadcasting live. Fumbles and false starts don't really matter; they can be taken out in the transcription. Hardly any disaster really matters; you can usually come back again and do it over. Relax and enjoy yourself; this is a grand adventure in talking and listening. It's likely to be enormously satisfying for both the narrator and you.

CHAPTER 3

Conducting the Interview

Whom to Interview

Whom would you *like* to interview? What are you interested in finding out? Do you know of anyone who might want to tell their story? These are the key questions to ask yourself as you set off in search of a narrator.

My own experience seems astonishing in retrospect. I had never heard of Septima Clark before I learned that she was waiting for me to come and interview her. A friend of mine, the writer and teacher Herb Kohl, made the arrangements. When he met Mrs. Clark he realized that she was longing to tell her story and that her story was likely to be very significant. He knew, from our personal conversations, that I was yearning to try my hand at writing biography. He also knew that I could identify with Mrs. Clark's background since I, too, had grown up in the South under segregation, and that I was trained in conducting historical research. He asked Mrs. Clark if I could come to interview her; when she consented, he returned to California and told me that she was waiting for me to come to South Carolina.

Herb's intuition made some important connections—that understanding Mrs. Clark's role in the civil rights movement would become so significant to me that I would find the energy to carry through the project, that telling her story to me would invigorate Mrs. Clark and that she would open herself up to deeper memories and insights than she ever had before. I would be an audience before whom she could make an honest analysis of her life.

You may have friends who can help you connect with the person you want to interview, or you may need to make your own connection. But the necessities are the same: a person who wants to tell his or her story (and this includes just about everybody) and a genuine interest on your part in what is being told.

Septima Clark was 81 years old when we made our initial fifteen hours of taped interviews. Later, her memory was no longer so sharp and clear. We were fortunate in that we came together at the right time.

That is something you should consider in choosing a narrator. If you want to write something historical, something about how people used to live or how to do something that is no longer done by many, you should choose an older person. People between the ages of 55 and 80 have lots of experience to describe and analyze; many are eager and able to do it. Individuals vary a great deal in their ability to recall; for many, the distant past becomes especially vivid as they grow older.

What Kind of Piece to Write

If you want to write full-length biography, you ought to interview someone who has lived a long time, but not so long as to lose clarity. You might interview one or both of your grandparents, or visit retirement centers, or find a couple celebrating their 50th wedding anniversary, or someone who is just about to retire.

But unless you are especially interested in whole lives, in how people get from one chapter of their lives to the next, then you probably will start with a shorter piece, focused on some specific part of a person's life.

You might start with a character sketch. For this you would choose an interesting narrator and see if you can write a piece in which he displays his character. You might choose a classmate or the chief of police. You might chose your school principal, custodian, or school board chairperson. You might choose a minister or musician —someone with qualities that you respect or dislike. You don't need to admire your subject, but it helps to have some kind of strong feeling.

Or, if you were interested in preserving some culture that is dying out, you could write a how-to-do-it story or how-it-used-to-be story. High school students in Rabun Gap, Georgia, have made a specialty of this and have published their stories in a series of books called *Foxfire*. Look at figure 4 for a sample of their story ideas, which are, of course, tailored to their community.

making and using a handmill for grinding corn

a corn sifter made of deerskin with holes punched in it with an awl.

making and using a gritter for preparing corn not yet dry enough for grinding.

"wild pounds" to put cattle overnight to protect them from bears.

building fires around fields at night to keep deer out

pre log house dwellings

pot racks (that hang inside fireplaces)

how to build a proper cooking and a proper heating fire

making and using a horse-mill—horses on a log treadmill that worked a set of cogs that turned millstones for grinding corn

cloth "bolters" to separate wheat bran from flour

making and using flails

horse-drawn threshing machines

coonskin caps, and clothing of animal skins

making and using a "flax-break"

also "tow" from flax (which is spun) and one-piece garments of flax

coverlet patterns

physical contests—lifting, funning, jumping, boxing

the pony express

making pack saddles and saddles

"lining" songs at church. "Common meter" versus "short meter."

how to become a witch

whipsaws (or two-man ripsaws)

existence of a family "bad man" to avenge wrongs done to his family

schools: schedules, subjects, grading systems, segregation of sex, teacher training, Millard's memory of kids all bringing one ingredient for a common pot of soup for lunch, games, contests, parents' days, etc.

clay holes

bark ropes for corded beds before rope came in

making turpentine (reference to a spot on Wolffork involving iron pot, rocks, etc.)

makeshift houses—such as "rock houses" boarded up in front expressions

House floor plans with placement of furniture etc. Traditional App. architecture.

mule freighters that kept stores and towns supplied with goods

peddlers and gypsies

crossbows made by boys

books available to homes—and found there—like *Pilgrim's Progress*

deathbed conversations and the resulting baptisms of the dying

burying people facing the sunrise? Making flowers out of crepe paper?

gold panning

muzzle rifle making—hog rifles, etc./plus bullet making, powder horns and flasks

Figure 4: Foxfire idea list

You might want to understand more about a major historical event by interviewing a person who lived through it. The closest you will get to such an event is to talk with someone who was there. You might interview someone who experienced the Great Depression, World War II, atomic tests, the establishing of the United Nations, or the assassination of John F. Kennedy. When you do this, "you are making what happened to him come back to life again," in the words of one high school student.

You might want to write a feature story about something that interests you in your community. In Rabun Gap, Georgia, an example of a feature story would be one about rattlesnake handling in church or about growing ginseng. In my community a feature story might be about California cuisine or what it was like being Japanese-American during World War II. Feature stories can be about anything and can be in the past or present.

You might want to write a personality story that features the character of the person you interview. You could choose a well-known personality in your community or a secluded person who has qualities you would like to portray.

Finally, you may want to tell your own story. In that case, you can be the narrator and find a friend to be the interviewer. You can even make up the questions for your friend to ask, but you will be the one to transcribe the tape and write from it. If talking is easier for you than writing, as it is for most people, this is a good way to write your own autobiography.

Once you have some notion of what kind of story you want to write from your interview, you are ready to proceed. Your idea will change considerably as you proceed, but you need to have some plan in mind in order to get started.

What to Ask

Now you can prepare some questions to ask your narrator. But before you think about making up questions, let me tell you my experience with questions when I interviewed Mrs. Clark.

I went armed with a long list of questions that I had prepared to ask her. But I never did consult that list during the interviews because I was too busy concentrating on what she was telling me. I found out that paying attention is very difficult work. After an hour and a half I was always dripping wet (the temperature was 95) and nearly exhausted, unlike Mrs. Clark, who was eager to continue. I concluded that listening well is much more important than consulting a list of questions, especially if your narrator wants to talk.

Nevertheless, it helped me to have prepared the questions. I reviewed them each night to remind me of what was missing from Mrs. Clark's narrative. Writing down the list made me think through what I hoped to get on the tape and gave me practice in generating good questions. Also, having the list helped me feel confident that I knew what I was doing.

So, before you start an interview, make a short list of general questions you would like to ask. You will need to personalize them when you are actually talking with your narrator. You can't just read them off the paper. You will have them in mind, so that you can ask them naturally when the time is right. After the interview you can check off the ones you covered and remind yourself to ask the others at the next interview.

Thinking of productive questions is not easy. Many adults have little skill at it and don't provide good models for you to learn from. It may take several years of practice to become skilled at this. But the time you spend practicing will pay off in richer satisfaction in almost any job you can imagine and in every human relationship, because questioning and listening is what we do all the time.

Here is one way to start. After you have decided whom you want to interview, write down ten reasons why you chose this person to interview. What is it about this person that interests you?

Here is the list I made for myself, saying why I chose to interview Mrs. Clark:

1. She helped start the civil rights movement.
2. She is black.
3. She is a woman.
4. A good friend asked me to.
5. She wanted me to.
6. She is involved in Highlander Folk School.
7. She is a teacher.
8. She grew up black under the system of segregation.
9. She figured out fast ways to teach adults to read.
10. She is a leader in social change.

Now take your list of reasons and develop out of it some questions to ask. For example, my list suggests these questions:

How has your life been different because you are black?

How has your life been different because you are a woman?

How did you find out about Highlander School? Why did you
   get involved there?
Why did you become a teacher?
What was it like to grow up black under segregation?
How did you figure out how to teach adults to read? Is your
   way of teaching different from other ways? How is it dif-
   ferent? Which way is best?
Do you see yourself as a leader in social change? Did your fam-
   ily see you as a leader? your friends? your colleagues?
   Martin Luther King, Jr.?

Analyze this list; discuss it with yourself or others. What ques-
tion(s) are likely to produce the most boring answers? Why?

I think that the question "Is your way different from other
ways?" would produce a boring answer—"yes" or "no." I followed
it with "How is it different?" to expand the yes/no answer. I could
have skipped the yes/no question, as I did in the first two questions
above, by asking "how" in the first place.

Notice that many of my questions start with "why?" Do these
usually produce interesting answers? Why?

Notice that at the end of the list I used questions to deepen the
material and get more perspectives on it. Here is the basic form:
How did you feel about _____? How did your parents feel? your
neighbors? your colleagues? your children? or whatever is appropriate. Don't make a catalog of it; just have the catalog in your head to
choose from.

Another way to look at your questions is to see if any of them
are "leading questions," i.e., do they lead your narrator to give a
certain answer that agrees with what you think, or with your expec-
tation of what the narrator thinks? If I had asked Mrs. Clark,
"Wasn't it terrible growing up under segregation?" I might have
steered her answer in a certain direction. She might, possibly un-
consciously, have tried to avoid conflict with me and out of polite-
ness tended to agree, even though her real feelings were more complex than that. Interviewers should refrain from indicating their
own opinions and expectations. Analyze your questions to see
whether they reveal your attitude; all too often they do.

If your question does not result in an interesting answer, it
probably wasn't a good question and needs to be followed up with
more questions. You don't need to accept a boring answer; find
ways to delve deeper into interesting material.

Here are a few samples of the type of questions that produce boring answers, followed up by questions that are likely to produce more interesting answers:

Did you enjoy growing up?
> What kind of things did you enjoy?
> What did you not enjoy about growing up?

What is your favorite food?
> Why is this your favorite food? Describe the occasion you first had it.
> How do you prepare it? What is your mother's favorite food? your grandmother's?

Where were you born?
> What was it like in Charleston when you were little?

Who did you marry?
> How did you feel about getting married? Why did you decide to do it?
> How did your parents feel about your doing it?

Don't be afraid to ask daring questions in order to get beyond the surface answers. This is not easy to do when you are questioning a person you hold in awe or who is much older than you are. But in an interview the usual roles for social conduct do not apply; you are likely to be rewarded for boldness. After all, the worst that can happen is that your narrator will become silent or say, "I'd rather not answer that question."

Here are a few possibilities; add some more of your own:
1. What comic strip did you like best as a kid? How did it affect you?
2. Who was your favorite hero when you were growing up?
3. Who had the biggest influence on you up to now? Who does now?
4. Under what circumstances did you first make love?
5. What was your narrowest escape?
6. What was your biggest mistake?
7. What are your five favorite activities?
8. What scares you most in life?
9. How do you want your funeral to be?
10. What do you want in your obituary?

Answers that are interesting include not just information, but also feelings and interpretations. What does your narrator's life mean to him or her? How does he or she make sense of it? What are the main themes? Here are some questions to ask that challenge narrators to reflect on their lives. Add some of your own.

What was the hardest thing you ever had to do?

What turning points do you see in your life?

What do you see as the best or happiest time of your life? What do you see as the worst?

If you had your life to live over again, what would you do that was different?

Do you see any great opportunities that you missed?

Did your life turn out the way you thought it would?

How are you different from your children? Do you think your children have a better life than you did?

How are you different from your parents? Do you think you've had a better life than they did?

Remember, these lists of questions prepare you to be ready to respond to your narrator. But during an interview, you keep the questions in the background and focus your attention as much as possible on listening to your narrator.

Practicing with Questions

Find at least one friend who will help you practice asking questions. Of course, you can do this in a group or in a classroom, where you break up into groups. Role-play an interview; one of you can be the interviewer and the other one the narrator. Others can watch and discuss what questions worked best. Then you can change roles and someone else can practice asking the questions.

Here are two situations you might want to role play:

1. You are interested in what the life of 5-year-olds is like. You want to understand kids of this age in this culture right now. It's been ten years already since you were five, and you've forgotten what it's like. Besides, the culture is always changing, and you want to see what current children are interested in.

2. You want to get to know your teachers (or your parents) better; you want to interview them about what they did when they were your age. Discuss with your friends what questions would be good to ask. Try these questions out on each other; see if they are productive questions, and see if you can spontaneously devise more for the ones that don't produce much of an answer. This may work best when your friend is role-playing a 5-year-old; when your friend role-

plays an older person, he or she will have to invent answers, not simply pull one out of memory.

After some role-playing, try out your questions on kindergartners, parents and teachers, using a tape recorder. After the interview, play back the tapes to a friend, or to classmates, and together analyze what went well and why, and what didn't and why.

By now you have realized that one obstacle to framing effective questions may be that you simply don't know enough to ask the right question. You need to do some research. Sometimes just winging it will not produce the quality of interview you want.

One practice situation might be to learn more about your grandparents. If they are not available, you can interview your parents about what they know about your grandparents.

Before you start framing questions, do a little research. Make a time line and get clear about when your grandparents were born, when they were in their teens, when they were in college or starting work. Then find out what was going on in the nation at that time, or in their region, who the national heroes of the time were, what the political issues were, what major inventions took place, etc.

Just for starters, here is a short list of inventions:

1916–17: candy bars and cigarettes
1917–27: number of telephones doubled
1919–29: number of automobiles quadrupled — 6 million to 23 million
1922: radio available
1927: movies with sound ("talkies")
late '40s: television available
1960: birth control pills available
1963: tape recorders on the market
1969: first person on the moon

Here are some sample questions for learning about the lives of your parents, grandparents, or teachers when they were young. Each question represents an area that needs to be developed with many other questions.

What kind of clothes did you wear?
What kind of toys did you play with?
What games did you play?
What chores did you do?
What was school like for you? What are your most vivid memories of school?

What pets did you have?

Where did you go for special outings?

What clubs did you belong to?

Describe going to church and what it meant to you.

What were your favorite books? Why?

What did you do on dates?

What do you remember about the family doctor?

What cars were popular? Which ones did your family own and why?

How much did things cost? How much did your father and mother earn? Were things cheaper compared to earnings then or now?

What do you remember about your wedding? How did you meet your future mate? Why did you decide to get married?

Another topic you might want to practice with is the Vietnam War. Perhaps you know some Vietnam veterans and want to understand better how that war is still affecting their lives. Your research might include seeing a movie like *Platoon* and making a list of questions it generates for you.

Reading a good children's book about a topic is always a good way to start your research. About the war in Vietnam you might read *Charlie Pippin* by Candy Dawson Boyd, which contains lots of factual background about the war.

After several years of interviewing, the high school students who produced the Foxfire books developed a sample list of questions to ask when they wanted to write a personality story about someone; here, in figure 5, is their list.

For samples of interviews, see appendix B.

Productive Interviews

Interviews are always unique and unpredictable events. Each one is the interplay of two personalities. Your task as an interviewer is to be sensitive to what is happening, so that you can help your narrator become as relaxed, talkative, and revealing as possible. An interview should be a monologue, not a dialogue; the narrator should do most of the talking, with the interviewer on the sidelines, encouraging and cheering on.

1. What were times like when you were a child?
   - How did you and your family live?
   - Were times better, or worse. Why?
   - What is your earliest memory?
2. What types of things did you do as a child?
   - What did you like to do most? Why?
3. How did your parents treat you?
   - What did they do with you that you remember best?
   - What times with them were the most enjoyable to you? Why?
4. What advice or training did your parents give you that has helped you to lead a better, fuller life?
   - What examples did they set for you?
   - How did you profit from them?
   - Do you feel your parents prepared you well for life?
5. As a teenager did your parents let you socialize with boys/girls?
   - Did you have "dates" as we call them now?
   - Where would you go when you went out?
6. What was it like when you first went out on your own?
   - Were times hard?
   - Did you marry?
7. What kind of work did you do to support yourself?
   - Was it difficult?
   - What did it mean to you?
8. How do you feel about living in the country?
   - How about the city?
   - Which do you like best? Why?
9. Do you feel there is a difference between country people and city people?
   - If so, what is it, what makes it so?
10. How big a part has religion played in your life?
    - What are your feelings on it?
    - Do you read the Bible? Should everyone?
    - What is your proof for your belief in God?
    - How has He shown Himself to you?
11. How do you feel about life in general today?
    - How different is it from the way it used to be?
    - Is the quality of life better or worse now?
12. Are people different from what they used to be?
    - In what ways?
    - Are these changes good or bad?
13. How do you feel about the youth of today?
    - Are the teenagers different now, from the way you and your friends are?
    - What has caused these changes?
14. What do you think of the direction our country is going in today?
    - Is America being run well, or badly?
15. What do you consider to be the most valuable possession you have ever had?
    (Something you *could not* have done without in your lifetime.) Why?
16. Have you done everything in your life you wanted or planned to?
    - If not, what were you not able to do?
17. If you could go back and live your life over, what would you change?
18. How do you feel about:
    - money
    - friendship
    - kindness
    - honesty
19. What do you consider to be vices, or faults, in people?
    - Why are these things bad?
    - How can they be overcome?
20. What advice could you give young people which would help them to lead better lives?
    - What experiences have you had that they could benefit from?

Figure 5: Foxfire questions list

If you are usually quiet, reserved, and good at listening, you may fall into the role of interviewer more easily than a person who is used to being a big talker. Such a person must keep a tight rein on his mouth when interviewing.

If your narrator is a big talker, your job as interviewer will be easier. If your narrator is quiet and shy, you may need to come back several times before he begins to feel comfortable. Follow his lead — maybe after he talks about something completely off the subject he will be ready to discuss what you have in mind.

Good listeners remind their narrators that they are right in there listening by making comments such as "Uh huh," "Really?" "Gracious!" "What next?" "Just what I need to know," "Go on." These non-directive comments are often better than questions; they keep your narrator going without steering his remarks in any particular direction.

To encourage someone to talk in greater depth, interviewers use questions like:

Can you give me an example of that?

Can you describe that in more detail?

Let's go back to _____. Tell me more about _____.

During the interview is not a good time to play the role of a know-it-all. You should admit right away when you are confused and don't understand, so that your narrator can explain. You may even set up some non-verbal ways of letting your narrator know when you are confused. One student interviewer nodded as the interview went along if the story was clear to her. If she stopped nodding, then her narrator knew at once that he needed to add more explanations.

Don't expect to be able to complete an interview in just one visit; plan to come back at least a second time. Even a professional can seldom get everything the first time. You will probably feel rushed; you don't know what you are looking for the first time. You and your narrator will both appreciate having time to reflect about what came up during the first interview, and during the second or third you will both be able to achieve greater depth.

Remember that interviews are unpredictable. Narrators will respond in ways that you didn't expect; surprising topics will emerge that suddenly seem more important than what you had planned. Go with these surprises—play detective—follow your instincts. You will be making unexpected discoveries right and left.

Or maybe you won't. The flow of an interview depends only partly on you and your questions. Your narrator plays a large part, too — and maybe the chemistry just won't work well between the two of you. Don't evaluate your effectiveness on the basis of one interview. If you feel too frustrated, try interviewing someone else.

Even if your interviews are going extremely well, some of your questions might be painful or discomforting to your narrators. Some aspects of their lives will be difficult to discuss. You can wait until you and your narrator know each other better before bringing them up. But some you can't predict. When your interviewer changes the subject or becomes less talkative, you may have hit a sensitive area. It is also a meaningful area that will prove important to your narrator and to your story. Drop it for now, but come back later from a different angle when you have established a closer trust.

You must exercise your own judgment about asking personal, sensitive questions that explore fears, mistakes, losses, unhappy events. Life has its dark side, and to leave it out is dishonest. Conflict, challenge, obstacles, tragedies — these are the times when a person's real spirit emerges. But we all have trouble discussing some things or even admitting that they have happened to us; they may seem too awful or disappointing even to acknowledge. By not being afraid of raising sensitive questions and by not passing judgment on what you hear from your narrator, you'll encourage your narrator to talk freely. You can accept whatever happened—it's simply what happened, and you know already that life is a lot more complex than anyone ever expected it to be.

One excellent way to improve your interviewing is to watch skilled interviewers at work. Watch interview shows on TV and analyze how the host/hostess does it. Listen to radio interviewers. Find a newspaper reporter or book reviewer who will let you accompany them on an interview. Watch a skilled principal talk to a student, or an admissions officer to a prospective student. (Doctors, psychologists, and psychiatrists are skilled at this, but their relationship to clients is confidential.) How about a kindergarten teacher interviewing a five-year-old, a lawyer or an architect with a client, a mother at the dinner table? The possiblities are endless, because in some sense we all interview each other every day: "Hi, how are you?"

In the San Francisco Bay area there are two businesses that provide taping and interviewing services to people who want to record their family history. One, called Remember When, collects family histories on audio tape. Its interviewer, Judy Maschan, encourages people to recall what they were doing during great moments of the twentieth century, from wars to earthquakes. In 1987, two one-hour tapes cost $70, each extra hour $30.

The other business is called Lifeline Productions. Its founder, Keith Thompson, videotapes a narrator—some legendary figure in a family—to create an heirloom-on-tape. Usually some other member of the family hires him to interview the narrator. In 1987, Thompson charged a maximum of $300 for five hours of tape, a minimum of $100 for one hour.

Is there such a business in your area? If so, see if you can accompany the interviewer to observe. If not, why not start one?

Practical Tips for Interviewing

Now it is time to get busy interviewing. Here are some tips on the specific steps that are part of the process.

1. Making Arrangements

Make a visit to your potential narrator to describe what you want to do and to solicit his cooperation. Narrators want to meet the person who will be interviewing them; they can't imagine what the interview will be like just by talking to you on the telephone. They want the assurance of meeting you face to face before commiting themselves to telling you about their personal lives. Talking on the telephone may not give them this assurance, and the chances are greater that they will say no if you try to make arrangements by telephone. Agree on the time and place for the interview, give them an idea of the topics you want them to talk about, and suggest about forty-five minutes for the first interview.

Describe how you intend to use your story and ask permission from your narrator. If it's for school, explain that you will be turning it in as an assignment to your teacher and that you will be sure the narrator gets a copy, too. (But not before you turn it in, unless he wants that condition.) Or if you want to publish it in any way— family copies, or in a school or community publication—then agree on the terms. The narrator should be able to review it before any publication. If you don't assure him that he will have this chance, he may be more inclined to censor himself as he talks.

If you would like to bring along a camera or a photographer to take photos, ask permission of your narrator. Or suggest that you would like to look at his photos and possibly choose some to copy.

Bring along all your equipment to this first visit when you are making arrangements. You and your narrator may not be able to wait, and you may want to get started on the spot.

2. Setting Up

Find an outlet to plug in the recorder, unless you are using batteries. Find a place to put the recorder between you and the narrator, so that the microphone can pick up both of you. Think about noise in the environment and find ways to avoid it. (See chapter 2 for more details about this.)

Try to minimize interruptions. Mrs. Clark and I had to record early in the morning because by 10 A.M. her telephone began ringing off the hook.

Find a place well away from other people. Having spectators doesn't work — they can't avoid jumping into the conversation. (Trying to interview two narrators also doesn't work; they often contradict each other and even argue. Do this only if both narrators were present at the same event you are investigating.) Make sure your narrator is comfortable; don't let him give you his favorite chair.

3. Interviewing

If you are interviewing as a team, one person asks the questions and the other watches the equipment and takes notes.

If you are interviewing alone, it's still a good idea to take notes, if you can manage. The main things to jot down are questions and topics that you want to come back to, or questions you didn't get to ask because you didn't want to interrupt.

It is also a good idea to jot down the names of people and places that the narrator mentions. That way you can check the spelling with the narrator after the interview.

Remember to let the narrator chat in a natural way. Don't hustle him along by rapid-fire questions. Ask only one at a time. Give him time to reflect. Silence is wonderful; use it to jot down a note rather than to leap in with another question. Usually the narrator will reveal the most sensitive material only after hesitating; if you rush in with a question, you will miss it.

Keep an eye on the tape and suggest a break just before it runs out. If the tape does run out while the narrator is still talking, just flip it over and ask him to repeat a few sentences.

4. Ending the Interview

Interviewing is tiring; stop before both of you are exhausted. Agree on a future time and place; plan with the narrator what topics you want to cover next.

Ask the narrator how he is feeling about the interviews. Is he enjoying them? Could anything be done to make them more pleasurable?

Sit down for a few minutes with your notebook and check the spelling of proper names with your narrator. This will make your job of transcription much easier. Also, take time now to make a quick sketch or a list of things in the setting where you are conducting your interview. You can refer to these notes when you write your introduction; you will be surprised how much easier it is to write when you have some written record—the more descriptive, the better. Use words as a photograph. If you have brought along a camera, a few pictures will supplement your narrative, but not substitute for it. Write while the scene is fresh.

5. Follow-up

After each interview, label the tape with the date, name of narrator, and the topics covered.

Listen to the tape. You may want to make an outline of the topics covered and certainly will want to jot down questions for the next interview.

Also, analyze the interview for what went well and what did not. Listen to your questions and see which ones got a full, satisfying response. Notice which ones seemed to shut off your narrator. As you listen to the tape, it will be easy for you to hear what kinds of questions are most productive.

Write out a full description of the interview setting, how your narrator responded, and how you felt about it all. Just pour this all out in writing as if you were talking to your closest friend—or say it to your tape recorder. Then you will have a record that you can edit and revise when you write your piece and want to introduce your narrator.

After the final interview, thank your narrator again for everything and say what it has meant to you. Give some estimate of how long it will take you to produce a typed record of the interview and remind the narrator of the terms that you both agreed to when you made initial arrangements.

As soon as you have a typed paper or a published article, deliver a copy to your narrator. He will be as excited as you are. If your narrator would like them to give to friends and relatives, you might offer to make or provide several copies.

Looking at Old Photographs

Look at the photographs on the following pages, then consider these questions:

1. What clues tell you that this picture was taken a long time ago? Look in the background as well as the foreground.
2. What is shown in the picture that you don't understand? Whom can you ask to explain it?
3. What do you notice about the way people are dressed? How are their clothes different from your clothes?
4. What is different about the way people are posed? What are they expressing with their body language? How is it different from your body language?
5. How has money changed since this picture was taken? What does that explain about the way some older people act about money?
6. How are the advertisements different from ads now?
7. How has transportation changed? How are buildings different — their materials and their style?
8. Can you imagine yourself in the photo? How would you have felt?
9. Do you respond differently to black-and-white photos versus color photos? How?

These questions can be used with any old photographs.

Figure 6: New York: 1938. Photo: Rudy Burckhardt

Figure 7: New York, 1947. Photo: Rudy Burckhardt

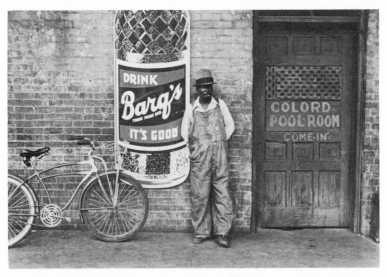

Figure 8: Montgomery, Alabama, 1948. Photo: Rudy Burckhardt

Figure 9: Georgia, 1948. Photo: Rudy Burckhardt

CHAPTER 4

Transcribing: From Sound to Paper

Transcribing is writing down on paper what you hear when you play back a taped interview. It's just plain work — slow, painstaking, nothing much glamorous about it. But there is some magic in it. In transcribing, you will capture on paper the unique qualities of the voice you have become familiar with. You will experience the mystery of little scratches on paper being able to convey and record the words and meaning of a human voice.

The scratches at your command are spelling and punctuation — letters, dots, and dashes. You will have many decisions to make — how far to bend standardized spelling in order to convey how your narrator actually sounds, where to start and end sentences and paragraphs, how to make sense of pronouns with unclear antecedents. You will get a better feel for how spelling, punctuation, and grammar help make sense out of words on a page.

But even excellent editing cannot make written speech sound like it does when spoken. The voice conveys nuances of inflection and emphasis that cannot be captured on paper, and the structure of oral stories often does not work as a structure for written ones. The task of the writer is to find a tone on paper that corresponds to the tone of the narrator's speech and to create a structure as effective as the narrator's oral one. For this reason, some oral historians argue that tapes should not be transcribed at all.

But if you want to write from tapes, you must transcribe at least some of the narrative. How much of it? That depends on your purpose and your experience. If you are just beginning to work with oral histories and your purpose is to write an assigned report for your teacher, maybe you won't need to transcribe everything. You can just listen to the tape, figure out what the narrator was trying to say, and put it down in your own words, transcribing just a few parts to use as quotations in your report.

But once you get some experience and your purpose is to write articles that feature the narrator, you should transcribe your whole tape, except for sections that are clearly not relevant or useful.

Who should do the transcribing? You. Even if you have plenty of cash to pay for assistance with transcription, suppress the temptation to hire someone. Doing it yourself will repay you with a better understanding of the written language. Besides, no one else can transcribe your tapes as well as you can. You were there at the interview. Since you asked the questions and understood the flow of talk, you will be able to fill in areas of the tape that are hard to hear or understand.

Do it now. Don't delay making the transcriptions. The longer you wait, the more you will forget and the harder it will become to make sense of your interview.

Unless you type well, you should make the transcription in pencil and type it later. It's enough to think about getting the words down, without thinking about what keys to strike.

It is worth buying a power pack for your recorder even if you use it only for transcribing. Otherwise, you will use up many batteries in the process.

You can save wear and tear on your recorder if you have an external microphone and use the off/on switch on it to start and stop the tape as you transcribe. If you have no external mike, you can use the "play" and "stop" buttons on the recorder, with lots of "rewind" to listen again. I did this four hours a day, for three months, and my machine did not give out.

It is difficult to estimate the time needed for transcription. This will vary with your skill and the sound quality of the tape. But be prepared for a long haul if you have several hours of tape. Professionals estimate six–twelve hours of transcription for each hour of taped recording.

Some recorders have the capacity to replay at a speed twenty percent slower than that of the recording. This feature certainly makes transcribing easier.

If you are very young or inexperienced with transferring speech to paper, you can do some of the work and find someone older or more experienced to help you out. Especially if your interviews have been about your family's history, probably someone in your family will be willing to help you.

Dialect or Standard English?

A big issue that you may have to deal with is the little matter of spelling. Are you going to put down your narrator's words in dialect or in standard English? Since we all speak more informally than we write, your transcript will not come out in strictly formal standard English. It will reflect spoken English, with looser constructions, ramblings, and run-ons.

If you interviewed someone who speaks something close to standard English with a basic American accent, this may not be an issue. You simply transcribe the words in standard spelling and punctuation.

But what if your narrator speaks black English or some other variation of standard English? Before you transcribe you will need to reconsider your purpose. Will your story focus on portraying a person, including his or her qualities of speech? Are you trying to preserve and display a particular cultural mode of talking? Or will you focus on the content of the interview, without emphasizing the personal style or cultural patterns of the speaker? Those who argue for the use of dialect feel that it is colorful, authentic, interesting, and rich, that it shows the inventiveness of people in creating expressions and culture. Dialect conveys a feel for a person that translation to standard English obliterates. Honoring dialect shows that people who do not speak standard English also have something worthwhile to say. Those who argue against transcribing in dialect say that it is much harder to read. They also point out that it may make the speaker sound foolish, untutored, country, backward — all put-downs in our culture. Standard English has become the standard against which people are measured.

A third possibility is some combination of standard and dialectical English. We all shift levels of diction constantly, as you will see when you transcribe.

Before you finally resolve this issue for your story, you might consider the wishes of your narrator. Will he feel put down if you permit non-standard spellings to stand? If he is a retired school teacher, you can bet he probably will. Not many people, unfortunately, are proud of their regional dialects. Dictionaries, schooling, and standard publishing have tended to undermine people's pride in the non-standard ways they speak. If you want to preserve your narrator's dialect, you may have to convince him of its value and beauty, and that you and whatever other audience will read his story are ready to treasure his particular way of speaking.

The issue here is standard or non-standard spelling, not grammar. Most oral historians agree that a person's grammar should not be changed. If a narrator says "I seen," the text should not be changed to "I saw." People's words are their own and belong to them; words cannot be changed without violating the spirit of the narrator.

My advice is to transcribe as closely as you can to the sound of the language, preserving whatever dialectical qualities it may have. You can decide later — in the editing stage — how much to shift to more standard spellings. Since it is much easier to edit toward standard form than to shift back to dialect, let the first transcription be as faithful as possible to the sound on the tape.

In my project with Mrs. Clark, one of my purposes was to portray her in her cultural context in as authentic and interesting a way as possible. This made it appropriate to use as black an English as I could get away with, which fit my own bias. I loved the sound of black English, since it resonated with my childhood memories of the black woman who took care of me. As I got to know Mrs. Clark, I came to treasure the different voices she spoke in, ranging from the Creole language of the sea islands to standard white English. I wanted my story to display her ability to speak all these variations of language.

Luckily, Mrs. Clark didn't mind having her words printed as she had spoken them. Luckily, too, I found a publisher who took pride and pleasure in Mrs. Clark's speech. I was able to keep the unique flavor of her speech all the way to the publication of my story, although I did standardize some of it for the sake of ease in reading.

Here is a sample of my initial transcript of the tapes with Mrs. Clark:

> S: . . . And then water was very scarce, so when you'd get through bathin yourself, then you could wash out your underwear in that same pan of water. If you had to wash your hair, you'd wash your hair in that same pan of water. Water was very scarce.
> C: How did you get it warm?
> S: From over the fireplace. They had kettles, black kettles, that you heated that water in. Tin tubs — that's what you bathed in. Most of the time they had a tin basin on that back porch, and this is what you washed your face in in the mornings.

53

C: And where did the fresh water come from?

S: There was a surface well. That's all they had was surface wells. That's one reason why so many people got sick, because there were no toilets, and when they went outside and used the bushes, when it rained, all that water drained into the surface wells, and that water was really impure.

Compare this with the published version (*Ready from Within*, p. 108):

> ... Water was very scarce, so when I'd get through bathing myself, then I would wash out my underwear in that same pan of water. During the week they had a tin basin on the back porch, and this is what you washed your face in in the morning.
>
> The water came from surface wells. That's one reason why so many people got sick, because there were no toilets. They went outside and used the bushes, and when it rained all that water drained into the surface wells. That water was really impure.

Tips for Transcribing

• Transcribe everything. Don't waste effort trying to decide whether or not to omit something; just put it down. Leave in the filler words — you know, the words people use in talking to give themselves a few seconds to gather their wits — or to check whether you are listening: "you know," "well," "you see," "yeah," "uh huh," "right?" Put them all down. Later, when you edit, you can decide how many to remove. Here in the transcript you want a record of everything that was said. After you have become an experienced transcriber and editor, you may be able to omit most filler words as you transcribe.

An exception to the rule above is a section of the tape that is clearly off the topic you will be writing about. If your story is about designing low–cost housing, you can omit the architect's digression about her trip to Australia last summer, unless it has something to do with low-cost housing. If you omit a portion, make a note in the transcript by using brackets: [The first ten minutes of side two were not transcribed. They contain a description of a trip to Australia.]

• Use brackets for any other description you may want to include: [clears throat], [laughs gently], [pauses five seconds], [mutters unintelligibly].

• Use the last names of the speakers if they are a reasonable length. Otherwise, use initials or some abbreviation. Using two sets of initials may make it hard to remember which one is the narrator; use some device, like "Mrs. C.," to distinguish the narrator from the interviewer.

• When you cannot make out what is being said, listen again. Try again later. Ask someone else to listen. Don't invent something; leave a blank in the transcript that can be filled in later. Go back and ask the narrator, if necessary.

• Forget about paragraphs. Experienced transcribers can put in paragraphs as they go along, but you and I are better off leaving that for the editing stage.

• When you finish transcribing by pencil, type the transcript. Make two copies of the typed transcript. One you will file as a permanent record of the interview. The second you will use to edit and write your story from.

• Audit your transcript; or better yet, ask a friend to. In oral history parlance, "auditing" means listening to the tape and checking it against the transcript to make sure that the transcriber heard and typed all the words correctly, did not add any extra words, and did a reasonable job of using spelling and punctuation to catch the meaning of the narrator. The sound of words can be deceiving. Here, from Willa K. Baum's *Transcribing and Editing Oral History*, are some examples of errors made in transcribing:

Transcription:	They used to have the *customers* sitting up with the dead.
Correct:	They used to have the *custom of* sitting up with the dead.
Transcription:	So the city had a *place*, and we had *other* places.
Correct:	So the city had *an appraiser* and we had *an appraiser.*
Transcription:	*They wouldn't send any money. Unless you ask the brother. . .*
Correct:	*Who asks anybody? The less you ask, the better.*
Transcription:	He was a *character, for sure.*
Correct:	He was a *caricature.*
Transcription:	I was appointed to the Task Force on *Economic Gross Inopportunity.*
Correct:	I was appointed to the Task Force on *Economic Growth and Opportunity.*
Transcription:	That was the first *raise in the marketing* agreement that went into effect.
Correct:	That was the first *raisin marketing* agreement that went into effect.

CHAPTER 5

Writing from the Transcript: First Steps

Now you have a written transcript in hand — the raw materials from which you will create a piece of art. Read through it once as if you had never heard of it before. How does it strike you?

Let's face it, probably parts of it are jumbled and boring. It may not hold your attention; sometimes you may wonder what the narrator really meant. What you have now is called a primary document — an unedited account by an eyewitness to the events of his own life. Left in this form, it would provide unstructured research material for future historians.

But you want to practice becoming a historian. You want to set the material in the context of other known information. You also want to create a story that will rivet someone's attention. You want a reader to keep turning the pages. You want to give your material a shape — a beginning, a middle, and an end. The transcript is completely malleable in your hands; you can chop away from it, add to it, and rearrange it any way that suits you.

There are many decisions to be made, and it is not even clear what order they should be made in. Remember that what you are doing is similar to carving a statue or painting a picture. You have to discover where the focus should be, how to arrange the elements, how to strike a balance of all the parts. This is not likely to be clear at the outset; it usually emerges only as you play with the material and rearrange it in various ways.

Try anything. Remember, you have an extra copy of the complete transcript. You can always go back to it, make a xerox copy, and start again with your editing. As you start to cut and paste don't be afraid; you will probably make several false starts and arrangements that don't suit you. This is what creation is all about—trying different solutions until you find the one that pleases you most.

First Editing

This first round of editing need not be drastic. Its purpose is simply to clean up the transcript so that it is easier to work with. (Eventually, as you become a skilled transcriber, you can perform this much editing as you make the transcription, thereby eliminating this step of the process.)

There are two tasks to perform in this initial editing: 1) remove the narrator's filler words and 2) remove the interviewer's fumbles and digressions.

The best way to learn to edit is to study some examples. Here's a sample of how I removed the narrator's fillers and the interviewer's fumbles from my interviews with Mrs. Clark.

The original transcript:

S. It was real funny. I think that I told you I met the sailor in Charleston. His ship left, and I just really didn't think I'd ever see him again. So the ship came back to Charleston, and when it came back I was up there teaching and somehow or other he found— he came up with the mailman. We didn't have bridges then. He had to come over on a ferry, and from the ferry with the mailman, and here he got up to—

C. On a boat or in a car?

S. The ferry boat brought him to Mt. Pleasant. When he got to Mt. Pleasant, he got in with the mailman who was coming up to McClellanville, and rode on up to McClellanville. So then we talked again, and he decided that he wanted to marry me. Somehow or other we both got that same notion.

The published version (p. 111):

Nerie Clark's ship returned to Charleston later on that spring. Somehow or other he found me. He came up with the mailman. We talked again, and he decided that he wanted to marry me. Somehow or other we both got that same notion.

Sequence

The next step is to get the interview in order, to get the sequence organized. You remember how, during the interview, you would ask the narrator to go back to some earlier incident or description and tell you more about it? Now you need to put this additional account with the first conversation on the same topic.

There are two basic ways to organize the material: chronologically and by topic.

If you're going to arrange it chronologically, you may want to use a time line (see Chapter 1 for information about time lines) as your organizer. If you are dealing with a long life, you could sort your manuscript by decades. Label little tabs of paper as follows and spread them out on a big desk or table

| 1900–10 | 1910–20 | 1920–30 | 1930–40 | 1940–50 | 1950–60 | 1960–70 |

Using a decade for each category works if your narrator has lived a long life. What if he is only twelve or fifteen? Then use one year for each category. You have to make your categories fit your manuscript.

Now read through your transcript and in the margin put the dates of the events described. If you don't know when an event occurred, you can relate it to other events you do know — it came *before* this and *after* that. Put a question mark beside passages you can't identify by decade.

When you have done your best at labeling the transcript, take scissors and cut it up, by decades. Stack each section under the label for its decade. Usually the text will come out in substantial chunks, but sometimes there will be one or two sentences that need to be detached from one category and moved to another category.

When every page has been cut up and stacked, tape the sections down on fresh sheets of paper in their new order.

The second method of organizing your material is by topics and sub-topics. For instance, when the *Foxfire* students interviewed Reid Chapman about his life, he did not describe events from each period of his life. Instead, he focused on what he loved to do — farming, fishing, and hunting. To organize a story about him, you might arrange his narrative into those categories.

If your story will be a how-to story, then the logical way to organize your transcript will be step-by-step. Write down a list of the steps involved and use those as your categories.

Maybe your transcript does not need reorganizing at all. Perhaps you planned your questions so carefully that everything came out in just the order you wanted. Or perhaps you want to show the reader exactly how the interview went. Or perhaps the character of your narrator is best exhibited by preserving the pattern in which the ideas came out.

I am accustomed to working with a typewriter, scissors, and scotch tape. I like to work with my material spread out before me on a large table so that I can literally see the whole structure take shape. If you are working in a similar fashion, you will need to decide whether or not to make a fresh typing before you go on to the next step. You may find it easier to work with a fresh copy, or you may feel that the cut-and-paste job is workable until you make the next decisions. If you are working on a computer, then of course all you need to do is to print out a fresh version. Be sure to save each version on disk.

Make an extra copy of your text at this point—a xerox of your cut-and-paste job or an extra printout. Save this copy to refer to in case you realize you don't like later versions and want to start afresh from this point.

Memorable Phrases

Right here in the beginning stages of your work, take time to have a little fun. Go through your transcript and hunt down memorable phrases, apt descriptions, eloquent expressions, surprising metaphors, unique combinations of words that only your narrator has ever put together. Write these in large letters on separate pieces of paper; tack them up to look at. Or buy yourself some sheets of "rub-on" letters (also called "transfer type" or "tack type") and make some little posters of eloquent expressions from your interviews. Later on, when your piece has taken some shape, you will find ways to use these memorable phrases as titles, subtitles, or captions. They may help you see what is most important in your interview, what the main themes are.

CHAPTER 6

Writing Short Pieces from Edited Transcripts

Now you have a transcript that is organized in some fashion, with the irrelevant material taken out. Keep in mind your simple purpose—you had a great experience interviewing an interesting person and you want to share that experience with your readers.

Review your whole interview. Which parts do you want to highlight? What should be the focus of your article? What was the point of your interview?

Types of Articles

Here are four possible ways you could organize your story: as a how-to article, as a personality story, as a how-it-used-to-be story, or as a feature article. Although these are only slightly different from each other, each provides a particular focus around which you can choose and prune your material.

• **A how-to article** is perhaps the simplest form because its structure must be step-by-step, from beginning to end. This book is an expanded how-to article; there is only one possible form for the structure—sequential steps. The trick in this kind of article is to provide all the information needed by the readers, with sufficient clarity so that they can carry out the activity described.

• **A personality story** features the character of your narrator. It uses anecdotes, incidents, and your narrator's choice of words to display his special qualities. Instead of your writing about him, "He was brave and generous," he tells stories about himself in which he reveals these qualities. A personality story need not go in a straight line, as a how-to does. Personality stories may zigzag back and forth from one topic to another.

 • **A how-it-used-to-be story** brings to life the olden days. It uses the narrator's descriptions of daily details to enable readers, whose daily experiences are very different from the narrator's, to imagine vividly a former time.

 • **A feature article** is about any event, activity, or festivity that goes on now or used to go on in your community. The story is organized around the event and may include accounts from several narrators.

Maybe when you planned your questions you were already certain about what kind of story you wanted. You asked questions that would reveal the personality or character of your narrator. Or you focused on how some aspect of life used to be. Or you featured some aspect of current life—what it is like to fish when there are oil rigs all around, what school is like for an immigrant student newly arrived, etc.

But interviews don't always turn out as you expect them to. Maybe you hoped to write a personality story, but instead your narrator produced a wonderful feature on what it is like to be a single father. This is your chance to reconsider what to focus on and what to omit or downplay.

Audience

Another aspect to consider is your audience. Imagine as clearly as possible who they will be, because who you think they are will influence how you write your story.

In telling Mrs. Clark's story, for instance, I wrote for young adults who might not be used to reading a lot. I assumed they did not know much about segregation or the civil rights movement. I knew that every place or idea mentioned needed to be explained, either by me or by Mrs. Clark, and that the whole story had to be interesting and written in short paragraphs that would be easy to read. If I had decided to write a scholarly book for university graduates who knew a lot about history, I would have written the book in a different way. I would have written about Mrs. Clark in the third person, instead of having Mrs. Clark tell about herself in the first person. I would have used footnotes, standard English, and longer sentences and paragraphs.

You need to make similar decisions. Who will read your story? Your immediate family? Your classmates and teacher? Maybe it will be published in a school journal or exchanged with another school. You might want to imagine an audience that you would *like* to write for, even though they won't actually have a chance to read your story — young people in the Soviet Union, for example. Will your readers be familiar with what you are writing about or should you assume that they know nothing about it at all?

Remember, compared to anybody else, you know a great deal about your narrator and the subject you have investigated. No matter who your audience will be, you know more than they do about your subject. In order to write effectively, you have to imagine what they need to know and how your story will sound to them.

You: In or Out?

Now that you have figured out a focus and an audience (you haven't written a word yet), you get to make another decision. What are you going to do with yourself in the interview? This one is fun because there are many possibilities.

One answer might be simply to leave you in the text as the interviewer. You might call it "An interview with So-and-so," write a brief introduction about the person, and leave in your questions just as they are, followed by the narrator's answers. This is a journalistic style often used in magazines. It is most effective when the interviewer's questions are quite elaborate and contribute a great deal to the flow of the interview. Sometimes it seems almost impossible to remove the questions without destroying the meaning of the interview.

Another method is to remove yourself entirely from the interview. With this method you make the narrator's story flow without interruption, as if he were telling the whole story without being questioned. With this form you remove the questions altogether. Then you connect your narrator's comments by inventing a few sentences that incorporate the sense of your questions and provide the transition from one topic to another. You yourself withdraw to an introduction, where you present your narrator, tell why you chose to interview this particular person, what the circumstances of your interview were, how you felt about it, etc. An example of this method is, of course, *Ready from Within*.

The most common way to solve this problem of where to put yourself is to use some combination of letting your narrator speak in the first person, while you write connecting passages in the third person (using the pronouns *he, she,* or *they*).

Here is an example of the transition I wrote for my story about Septima Clark. The parts spoken by her (in the first person) are held together by a third-person narrative written by me. In the final form my story took for publication, I decided to let Mrs. Clark talk uninterrupted by any comment from me. You can study the following passages to understand an alternative form, one that is effective for short articles:

Mrs. Clark considers that her old age began in about 1970 when, at the age of seventy-two, she officially retired from her work with the Southern Christian Leadership Conference.

In April 1970 Mrs. Clark gave her last workshop at the center in Dorchester, Georgia. She was ready to give up her constant travels. So much had been accomplished that she did not feel as if she were abandoning anything. And her sister, Lorene, was not well. She had developed Parkinson's disease and needed the daily care of someone who lived with her.

The SCLC put on a gala banquet for Mrs. Clark's retirement on June 19, 1970. Four hundred people gathered at the Francis Marion Hotel in Charleston to honor the woman who had laid the unseen groundwork for the civil rights movement. They gathered in one of the best hotels in the city, right on that Union Square where Septima Clark had hauled water as a girl, being careful not to walk on the sidewalks of houses belonging to white people. As Mrs. Clark said with mischievous eyes, "The air has finally gotten to the place where we can breathe it together."

At the banquet Mrs. Clark's colleagues presented her with their coveted Martin Luther King Award. The two-foot plaque bore this inscription: "To Septima Poinsette Clark for Great Service to Humanity."

Just four years before she retired, Mrs. Clark bought a new home. She explains the reason why:

WHILE I WAS WORKING with the Southern Christian Leadership Conference, my sister was living in the house on Henrietta Street that I had bought in 1927. It was on that same one-block street where we had grown up. I loved that old house—it had six large rooms of varying sizes. Three were strung out in box-car fashion, with three more on top of them. Each room opened onto the piazza, the long narrow porch that ran along one side of the house.

But the neighborhood had become unsafe. It got to the place where the boys down the street wouldn't let our mail stay in our mail box because my sister was at school teaching all day and I was away. When the mailman would come with checks, the boys would take them out.

One night I was in Minnesota. The American Friends Service Committee had sent me to a little town right out from Minneapolis, Minnesota, and while there I called my sister. She said she didn't want to talk because boys were taking hubcaps off the automobiles of the people who were in church. She was afraid that if she would call the police, the boys would come and do some harm to her. When I came home from there, I noticed that she was taking the carving knives upstairs with her at night. She was afraid someone would break into that kitchen (it was right on the yard) and would take the knives and do her some harm

I felt that rather than to live with fear like that, it is better to try to move. I wanted a home in a neighborhood I thought would be a little bit more safe, because I was still traveling, and my granddaughter was here going to school. I looked about two years before I found this house about two miles north of Henrietta Street in a middle-class neighborhood. We moved in here two days before Christmas, 1966. I was coming from Camden, Alabama, and everything was so clean we could just have our Christmas dinner and enjoy ourselves.

I was sixty-eight years old, and a whole lot of people said to me that buying a house was too big an undertaking at my age. But I tried it anyhow. I sank all my money in this house. It was aged, so I had to have lots of work done on it. Some people will go under with repairs like I've had, but I really trust in God and feel that I'm coming out. I just knock on lead at times. Money never did worry me much. I never had much, so I just made whatever I had do.

The problem of money became more acute for Mrs. Clark after her retirement. She had a little Social Security built up because the United Church of Christ had paid into it for her. But when she was teaching, her retirement funds had been put into a state pension, and the state took all that pension away when she was fired.

In 1976 the National Education Association started airing her case all over the United States. They believed she had been unjustly fired and unjustly deprived of her pension. In 1976 the legislature of South Carolina voted to restore her pension, and every year after that they sent her a check for $3,600.

Steps in Shaping Your Work

1. Choosing the Pieces

You have decided what kind of piece you want to write and you have a good idea of its audience. It is time to cut and paste again. You might want to use a long roll of paper here. Roll out a long strip and arrange your narrative on it. Cut out sections of the narrative that are off the subject or would bog down the story. Don't be surprised if you have cut out as much text as you've kept. What you leave out is as important as what you include. It is a matter of balance and timing. Your story has to move along fast enough to keep your reader's attention. This usually means that you will have to omit some material that you dearly love, but if you are honest, you know that it just doesn't fit in this story. (Maybe you can make another story of it.) Leave spaces where something has been omitted or where you need to add some explanation or comment. Tape or staple your sheets to the shelf paper (or to fresh sheets of $8\frac{1}{2} \times 11''$ paper), leaving spaces for transitions and wide margins for notes.

2. Writing Transitions

Your piece will probably need transitions. Now is the time to write them. Just explain whatever your reader needs to know to understand what the narrator is talking about.

Give your story to a friend or parent. Ask them to make a check anywhere they get confused as they read. When they finish, let them explain why they were confused, and you will know what you need to add or clarify.

3. A Beginning and an Ending

Now it is time to write a beginning and an ending.

There are several ways to begin a short article:

• Start with your narrator speaking for a paragraph or two, then enter with some description of who he is.
• Start with a description of the setting where you interviewed your narrator.
• Start with a thumbnail sketch of your narrator's life.
• Start by telling why you wanted to interview the narrator.

• Start with a straightforward description of how you got started on this piece and what you did to carry it out.

If your piece has taken the form of an interview, in question and answer format, or if it has taken the form of the narrator speaking without interruption, then your beginning will probably be some kind of separate introduction in which you present your narrator to your reader. This might include any or all of the last four techniques above.

Here is an excellent example of a Foxfire student's introduction for a personality article about Hillard Green:

> Essentially [his house] is a room with a roof on it. The wooden floor is bare and unwaxed. There's no ceiling—it's open to the ridgepole except for places where planks have been laid on the joists to provide a storage area above. A wood stove, a battered sofa, an ancient double bed, a table covered with an oilcloth, and a stiff-backed chair are the basic furnishings. Throughout the room, however, one spots the little details that make it home: the sardine can nailed to the wall for a soap dish; the neat stack of wood beside the stove; the horizontal poplar pole on which a clean pair of overalls and a dishtowel hang; the axe, pile of onions, and canned tomatoes and cucumbers under the bed; the garden tools and walking sticks over beside the door; the kerosene lamp; the outside door pull made of a discarded thread spool and the inside one made from the crook of a laurel bough; the bucket and dipper for cold water from the spring; the mop made of a pole with a burlap sack tied to the end— all these things label the house as Hillard's and make it his alone.
>
> (*Moments*, p. 33)

Now take a look at my introduction. Since it introduces a book-length narrative, it can be much longer than one for a short article. Make an outline of my introduction to identify the topics that I covered. Notice that I began rather obliquely by talking about my own childhood to explain what segregation was and why I was interested in Mrs. Clark's life. If I were writing an *article* about Mrs. Clark instead of a book, I might use only part of my introduction.

Now for an ending. You could:
• let the narrator have the last word. End with some particularly wise or moving passage that sums things up, moves to a crescendo, packs a punch, brings the story to a close. For an example, see the last paragraph of *Ready from Within*.
• let the narrator have the last word by simply stopping the conversation.

- have the last word yourself by explaining to the readers what are the lessons to be learned from your narrator, why the topic of the narrator's account is significant.
- describe the end of the interview and your departure.
- describe how you feel about the scene, the narrator, the topic, or the end of the interview.

Here are some sample endings. These are taken from *Salt*, a cultural journal published by students in Kennebunk, Maine:

> Now this cold March morning has turned into a cold March night. We got into the wharf about 7 p.m. By the time we got the shrimp and fish on the trucks it was close to ten.
>
> •
>
> "Motion has been made and seconded for $4,200 for the town dump. All in favor, please manifest by raising your right hand. And those contrary minded? And by your votes, you have so voted to accept it. And I so declare it."
>
> The time was fast approaching 11:30. We had been there since 7:30 and had experienced four hours of "Democracy in Action."
>
> •
>
> It had only taken us about two hours to find the honeybees. Monty said this had been an easy hunt. "I've only found about three more swarms any quicker than that." As he had explained, sometimes it took as long as two weeks.
>
> "If you was going to get the honey out of that, you'd have to cut down the tree, then take the saw and saw into it below and above that hole about half way through it, and take an ax and split the pieces out and tip 'em up and get the bees out that way.
>
> "When the people used to find a swarm of bees in the old days, it was an unwritten law that if you left your initials on the tree nobody else would touch it. They might find it, too, but if there's someone's initials on it, why they'd leave it alone.
>
> "Why don't we put the old-time law into effect and we'll carve the initials in the tree?
>
> "I'll tell ya'. We'll put an S on it for *Salt*, how's that?"
>
> •
>
> "I had one a week ago. Dr. Townsend's Sasparilla. It's about an eighty dollar bottle. It's really a beautiful bottle. It has a crack in it, but the rarity of the bottle still dictates a price of probably a ten to fifteen dollar bottle even though it has a crack.
>
> "It's a beautiful bottle, I think."
>
> Ted began to talk about his ink bottles. "See you can collect hundreds of ink bottles and never see the same one. They're all different, different colors, different shapes, different sizes. It's really a collection by itself."

Then he paused. "You'll be here all night once I get started. I just don't know how to stop..."

We had to leave, but we left with a knowledge of old bottles we didn't have before. Ted showed us that there is more to the bottle than the bitters inside.

4. Choosing Photographs

No matter how complete your descriptions, a photograph conveys something words can't. Select one or more from those that you took or from those collected by your narrator. If you want to use one of your narrator's, you will need to reproduce it, either by high quality xerox or by a professional photographer.

Decide where the photos should be placed in your article and write captions for them. Study them carefully for new questions that they may raise; go back and talk again with your narrator, if possible. My editors suggested that we put a photograph of Septima Clark on the back of the book, one that shows her laughing after living through so much turmoil.

5. Editing Your Article

Now your piece of art has emerged with a beginning, a middle, and an end. Congratulations! It has been hard work, and you should feel proud. Rest on your laurels and put it away for a few days, or a few weeks if you can. Then you can come back fresh to the final steps of polishing and honing.

A. *Make a copy and file it away* in case you want to return to this stage to begin again. Even better, make several copies, and pass them out to friends and relatives—representatives of your audience. Ask them to tell you what they like and don't like about your piece. Their suggestions might be very helpful. Most people like to help edit, especially if the piece is not their own writing.

B. *Read through for sequence, balance, and timing.* Is some part in the wrong place? Where could you move it? Is there a gap that needs to be filled—either by you or by your narrator? Does some passage, engaging as it might seem to you, need to be taken out because it is off the topic?

If you find any of these problems, cut and paste again. Remember, you have a copy in safekeeping in case your decisions make it worse instead of better.

C. *Now read through your article for transitions.* Have you explained everything your reader needs to know? Pretend you are an eager young person who has never been to your part of the country. Would everything in the story be clear to you? Write more complete transitions where they are needed.

D. *Next, read through your article for dialect.* You have to make your final choice now about how dialectical you want your narrator to sound. Consider your narrator — how he wants to appear in print. Consider your readers—how much dialect they know. Consider yourself—what do you prefer and why? Dialect may not be a question for you at all, since people are speaking in a standard way more and more.

E. *Now read your article with an eye for paragraphs.* Paragraphs play a large role in how readable your text is and what gets emphasized.

You may have been taught that effective paragraphs should follow one model: they should start with a topic sentence, which should be followed by two or three sentences that fill in with detail the idea of the topic sentence. But that is not how paragraphs work in the real world. There are no simple rules to describe what is best, and there is not one standard way. Paragraphs come in all sizes and forms; the same material can be paragraphed in several different ways, all of which work.

Start by analyzing your paragraphs. How long are they? Are they all about the same length or are some very short and others very long? Play around with your paragraphs. If they all tend to be short, try to combine some to make a few long ones. If they are all long, you can make it much easier on your reader if you break them into shorter ones, sometimes even just one sentence.

The best advice l have ever seen about paragraphs comes from Pamela Wood's *You and Aunt Arie: A Guide to Cultural Journalism Based on Foxfire and Its Descendants in the U.S. and Abroad.* Take a look at it in figure 10.

F. Can you stand to *read your story one more time?* Put it away again if you need a rest. Remember that serious writers are distinguished by their willingness to revise their manuscripts over and over. They don't get it all right the first time either.

This time watch for pronouns and what they refer to. In talking, people play rather loose with pronouns and sometimes throw them around without being clear about what the pronoun refers to. Sometimes the listener can figure it out from the general context.

In writing, pronouns without a clear antecedent can cause a lot of confusion. What is an antecedent? It is the noun that the pronoun is substituted for, that it refers to. The grammatical rule states

Break your story into pieces that the eye can swallow.

Okay, so that's another way of saying you should divide your story into paragraphs. Time and time again kids say, "I don't know how to make paragraphs." Let's take a new look at this whole business of paragraphing. It's one of the most overfeared parts of writing, a mole hill that's been treated like a mountain.

If you keep in mind why you are carving your story into paragraphs, it will come easier for you. You're not doing it because some composition book says to. You're doing it because of kindly impulses toward your reader, to help him read your story.

Let your eye run over a long unbroken column of type. Pretty awful, isn't it? The last thing you want to do is struggle through all that.

Now break the same column of type into paragraphs. Just break it the best way you can. Paragraphing is a matter of personal judgment. You and I might break this column in different ways—for equally good reasons. So don't get yourself all tied up in knots thinking there is only one "right" way to form a paragraph.

Here's one way that column of type might be paragraphed:

Here's another way it could be broken:

If you break it the second way instead of the first, you get a different emphasis because the first words of any paragraph stand out more than the other words.

You also get a different sense of how fast you're moving. Shorter paragraphs give you a feeling you're moving faster than long paragraphs do. Longer paragraphs have a more leisurely feel, as if you've got all the time you need to follow an idea around, or listen to a story, or argue a point.

So the length of your paragraphs might depend on the mood you want to create at the moment. And you might use paragraph length to change the pace of your story—to suddenly speed it up, with quick snappy paragraphs; or to slow it down and let it amble, with longer paragraphs.

Paragraphs are kind of fun to fool around with, once you get over the idea that there's only one right way to do them.

Just remember that you're paragraphing for the same people you wrote your story for in the first place, Sunny Stevens at the Sunoco Station, Mary Durgin at the liquor store, your mother, your cousin down in Texas, your friend. Do them a favor and make it easier for them.

You're scared. Good. If the idea of writing your first story for publication scares you, maybe you'll take a fresh look at this business we call "writing." You know what writing is? It's just plain labor, like hoeing potatoes or tuning a motor or painting a wall.

When you write something that's worth reading, you work up a sweat, a good honest sweat. But don't back away. There's nothing hallowed about writing.

If you can make someone listen to you while you're talking, you can make someone read what you write.

You're scared. Good.

If the idea of writing your first story for publication scares you, maybe you'll take a fresh look at this business we call "writing."

You know what writing is? It's just plain labor, like hoeing potatoes or tuning a motor or painting a wall. When you write something that's worth reading, you work up a sweat, a good honest sweat.

But don't back away. There's nothing hallowed about writing. If you can make someone listen to you while you're talking, you can make someone read what you write.

Figure 10: Paragraphing advice

70

that a pronoun must refer to some specific noun, namely, the particular one that immediately preceeds the pronoun. The pronoun cannot refer to some noun that comes before the last noun. In other words, the noun that the pronoun refers to should appear shortly before the pronoun, so that the reader can be sure who the "he," "she," or "it" really is. But in conversation some real doozies appear. Take the example in figure 11 (from Willa Baum's *Transcribing and Editing Oral History*, pp. 45-6).

Just check your manuscript to be sure that you don't have any *he's*, *she's*, or *they's* floating around not tied down to a specific noun. If you do, replace them with a noun or with a clear antecedent noun. If you can't be sure of the meaning, go back and check with your narrator.

6. Writing Captions and Sub-titles

Pull out the group of memorable phrases you culled as one of your first steps (see "Memorable Phrases" in chapter 5). Find phrases that please you and use them for a title and for sub-titles to the various sections of your piece.

7. Final editing and proofreading

You will need to make a few final readings to check punctuation and spelling. Ask your friends and relatives for help with these details. If you are using non-standard spelling to convey local variations in speech, then a computer program with a spelling checker will be of no use.

When I was ready to submit my manuscript to the publisher for the last time, after I had combed it repeatedly for errors in spelling and punctuation, I asked an English teacher to read it over. She found twenty-one errors in my introduction alone!

It is difficult to do the final copyediting—the nitty-gritty editing of spelling and punctuation—on your own manuscript. You, as the writer, are appropriately much more interested in the ideas, the flow, the structure, and the tone, than you are in the letters and specks on the page. They simply escape your notice. Ask someone else to help you copyedit your manuscript; you can provide them with the same service in return.

"He always gave us a little spending money. He always wanted to
spend it right away because he knew he'd talk him out of it if he
didn't."

From previous statements the editor marked it as follows:

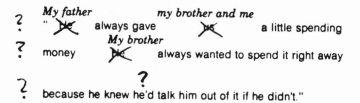

The narrator added "Cousin Bill" for the next to the last "he." In
the final typing it was typed without brackets as the additional
information had been approved by the narrator and there was no reason
to retain the original unclear speech.

If, however, the narrator had not reviewed the transcript, then
the editor's clarifications would have been added in brackets to alert
the reader that this was only an educated guess.

"[My father] always gave [my brother and me] a little spending
money. [My brother] always wanted to spend it right away because
he knew [Cousin Bill] would talk him out of it if he didn't."

Figure 11: Revision example

CHAPTER 7

Writing Full–Length Biography

Now you have already written a short piece or two from oral interviews. You have gotten the hang of it; you enjoy it; now it seems rather easy. You like the way it helps you get to know other people. You are learning about history, character, the real world, the art of writing. Now you want to undertake a longer piece, a full-length biography that will give you a chance to explore the details of a person's life.

If you are eager to do this, but the work seems somewhat overwhelming, remember that you do not need to work alone. Find a friend, or several, who want to work on this project. All of you can conduct the interviews, then each of you can transcribe part of the tapes. Construct a time line of the person's life, divide it into periods, and assign different parts to each other for adding background information and writing. You will need to work closely together, for part of the challenge of writing a life is figuring out what holds it all together.

The issues that come up in writing an extended biography are the same as those in a personality story, except they are larger and more complex. I will assume that you have read all the previous chapters of this book; my comments here will supplement that material by covering the special challenges of an extended oral biography.

Whom to Interview

This question assumes even more importance in an extended biography, because you have to care a great deal about this person in order to sustain enough energy to complete the project. Choose a person who wants to tell his story and enjoys providing details. If you have to drag it out of him, it will get to be a drag. Fortunately, almost everyone likes to talk about his own life.

Choose a person of appropriate age, someone who has lived long enough to have a full, complete life, but not so long that he is no longer able to remember it coherently. How I wish that I had interviewed my grandmother twenty or twenty-five years ago; now she is ninety-nine, and it is too late.

Choose someone others are interested in, or would be, if they only knew. This might be a grandmother who is loved and respected by a large family. It might be a pioneer in your community who influenced local development. It might be a retiring teacher cherished by generations of successive classes. It might be someone with an unusual occupation or a member of an ethnic group whose world view and customs are dying out. It might be anyone, but you are the one who needs to see what is interesting about that person, and who the audience of interested readers might be.

What Questions to Ask

If you want to write a full-length biography, then you will need to generate information about all the basic aspects of your narrator's life. The whole process of asking questions becomes much more complex, but you will have many interviews in which to explore all these areas.

Here is a list of some of these basic subjects:

birth	dating	travel
parents	dreams	politics
early childhood	choice of career	interests
schooling	education	illness/health
discipline	work	church
chores	religion	retirement
money	sex	death and old age
high school	marriage	visions
activites	children	

There are ways to focus a full-length biography that limit it in order to achieve greater depth and clarity on one set of issues. For example, you might write an intellectual oral biography that deals with the development of your narrator's thinking and leaves out details of personal life.

Another way oral biography can be focused is on political activities and consciousness, from the political left, right, or in between. For example, members of the Radical Elders Oral History Project worked together to document the ideas and actions of people committed to ideas considered "radical" or leftist on the American political spectrum. Here is the list of general questions used by that project. Notice that most of these questions are not "leading questions"; that is, they properly refrain from suggesting to the narrator what the interviewer thinks or wants to hear. Question 41, however, violates this guideline for effective questions.

RADICAL ELDERS ORAL HISTORY PROJECT
General Questions
1. When and where were you born?
2. What is your national ancestry?
3. If you immigrated to America, when?
4. What were your parents' class backgrounds?
5. Were they class–conscious? If so, in what way?
6. What were your parents' occupations?
7. Where were you raised?
8. Were you raised in a religious family? If not, were your parents religious?
9. Did you receive religious instruction as a child?
10. Were your parents politically active? Describe.
11. Describe your childhood. What events stand out in your memory?
12. Were you close to your mother or father? Describe your relationships with them.
13. Did you have any brothers or sisters? What were they like?
14. Where were you educated as a child? What were the most important things you learned?
15. Did your parents help you in your schooling? Describe what they did to help.
16. Who were your heroes as a youth? Why?
17. Were you conscious of world events as a youth? Describe what stands out in your memory.
18. What traditional values did your parents teach you that shaped your view of the world?
19. Did you get a diploma or certificate from school?
20. If you did not continue your formal education, what work did you do?

21. Did you enjoy working? Describe.
22. When did you become politically conscious? Describe.
23. What political groups did you associate yourself with? Describe them.
24. Were you aware of such groups as the Socialist Party, the Communist Party, the NAACP? In what way?
25. Where were you working and living when the Depression occurred? Describe how you survived during the Depression.
26. Did the Depression influence your political direction? If so, in what way?
27. Did you work in the WPA or other New Deal programs? Describe.
28. What mass organizations did you participate in during those years?
29. Did you join any political groups during the '30s? Describe.
30. How did you integrate your personal and political life during those years?
31. Were you involved in the CIO drives of the late '30s? If so, describe.
32. Did you sense that a war against fascism was a likelihood? Did you join any anti-war groups?
33. What were your reactions to the militarization of Germany, Italy, and Japan?
34. What were your reactions to the Soviet-nazi non-aggression pact?
35. Where were you when Pearl Harbor was attacked? How did that affect your political outlook?
36. Describe your activities during the war years. Were you politically active? In what way?
37. At the end of the war, did you anticipate an anti-Communist offensive emerging?
38. What were your political activities after the war?
39. Did you participate in any of the third party movements? Describe.
40. Describe your life during the Cold War years. Were you blacklisted?
41. When McCarthy launched his campaign of terror, how did you have to reorganize your day-to-day life?
42. Did you have to sign a loyalty oath?
43. Did your children understand what was going on?
44. What was your mass work during the '50s?

45. What were your political activities during the '60s? Describe.
46. What are you active in today?
47. Have your children followed your example in radical politics? Describe.
48. In retrospect, what stands out as the most important activity you have been in as an American radical? Why?
49. What lessons have you learned that would be helpful to the current generation of radicals in America?
50. What do you see in the future for American radical politics?
51. What is the meaning of radicalism, in your opinion?

In real life, every aspect of living is related to every other. For me, biography should include as much as possible, so that the reader can reflect on the interrelationship of different aspects. The real meaning emerges from the whole. I tried to do this with Mrs. Clark's story, and she agreed that it should be done this way. But writing oral biography is closely related to autobiography. Since you are helping narrators write their autobiographies, you must respect their wishes about what to include and what to omit, what the main focus will be.

Whose Point of View?

How people look at their lives may change over time. That in itself is part of their story, because it shows they are changing and developing. Some people don't change their interpretation of their lives; it stays pretty much the same throughout their lifetimes. I became aware of this process when I showed parts of Mrs. Clark's story to people who had known her at earlier stages of her life. She was eighty-one when I interviewed her. Her associates said of her account, "But that is not how Septima felt when that happened. I know, because I was with her and heard her talk about it then."

I felt confused by this response. I wanted our story to be accurate. Finally, I realized that it would be accurate in the sense of portraying Mrs. Clark at age eighty-one and how she interpreted her life then. The women's movement had shifted her analysis toward the feminist perspective. This story had to be her interpretation, and no one else's.

This problem is, of course, the proverbial one of the five blind men examining different parts of an elephant to describe what an elephant really is. Human beings are blind in that none of us can perceive the whole truth about reality. Each person sees a part of reality through the modes of seeing devised by his culture and through his own personal experience.

When you are writing oral history, you are up against these fundamental questions: Is it really true? To whom is it true? Are the facts accurate? Does it matter? What kind of history is it?

The basic decision you must make is whether to pass judgment on your narrator's account or to let it stand. The account is true to your narrator, and whether it is true in some other sense may not matter much. It is not a lawyer's brief or a sociological treatise; it is not even an objective history. It is a personal account of a personal truth. It may make a contribution to objective history, but someone else will evaluate that later; that job is not up to you.

However, you may discover through your research that your narrator has made a mistake about a date or a name or a place, and you may both agree that it should be corrected. But all interpretations must be your narrator's own particular, special version of the truth.

In the case of *Ready from Within*, both Mrs. Clark and I wanted it to serve as an accurate introduction to the objective history of the civil rights movement. So we were attempting two things at once: an objective account and a personal account. The lines were sometimes a little blurred, but we worked in agreement that the final version must be objectively accurate in its reference to major events.

There are ways to add other perspectives to that of your narrator. Suppose I were writing an oral biography of my grandmother. A major section would focus on her description of married life on a dairy farm in southern Wisconsin. Her four children grew up there; each remembers it somewhat differently. I could intersperse her account with theirs, to give additional information and other perspectives on the same experience.

A good example of this method is Al Frazer's oral biography of Dizzy Gillespie, the great jazz trumpeter. Frazer lets Gillespie talk about two-thirds of the time, but Gillespie's accounts are broken up by the voices of his wife, friends, or associates giving their versions of the same experience.

But even when you add other voices to that of your narrator, you should be scrupulously careful to keep out your own judgments and interpretations, except by the unavoidable decision of what you leave in and what you omit. If you find that you cannot resist interpreting your narrator's life, then perhaps you should make it clearly your own and write it in the third person. The oral interview will still be the main source of your information, but you will take control of the interpretation and emphasis. You might write completely in the third person and your narrator would not speak at all. Or you might write partly in the third person and partly in the first person of your narrator, deciding how much to let her speak directly.

Explaining the Background

In a lengthy oral biography, there are bound to be many references to events, places, people, organizations, and ideas that are no longer current. Your reader is going to need lots of help, and your narrator, who is completely at home in the past, is likely to forget that.

The first way you can deal with this problem is to make a list of every reference your narrator makes to a person, place, organization, book, event, or anything else you don't understand. As soon as you can, without interrupting the flow of the story, ask the narrator to tell you more about the items you've listed. If your narrator can provide the background, you won't have to look it up later. Some items you will have to research further, through other people, maps, books, newspapers, and photos.

Once you have collected background information that your narrator did not provide, you face the problem of how to get it into the text. Here are some solutions:

- Put it in your introduction.
- Write an introduction to each chapter, setting the context.
- Put brief information in brackets next to the item in the text.
- Make a footnote and put the information at the bottom of the page.
- Write a glossary of terms and put it at the end of your narrator's account.
- Make a chronology for the beginning or the end.
- Invent lines for your narrator to say that include the necessary information.

What Sequence to Use

This problem becomes complex in a full-length biography because there are so many options. Here are some basic ones:
- Start with the beginning and proceed chronologically to the present.
- Start with the most dramatic event, then flashback to bring the life up to that point, then proceed to the end.
- Start with a dramatic event, then alternate flashbacks and flashforwards.
- Focus on one period of the life, with other periods omitted, condensed, or summarized.
- Start with your narrator as he is now, with the rest of his life as a flashback leading up to the present.

Maybe it would help if you drew a time line so that you can study your options visually. I didn't do this with *Ready from Within*; I muddled through four different versions before I visualized what I was doing. Here are the four options I tried:

• Birth to present: This seemed the normal way to write a biography, but it didn't work because it proved too boring for the reader to go through all of Septima's childhood without knowing what she did as an adult.

• 1956–70; 1898-1955; 1971–present: This started her life at its most dramatic moment, when she was fired.

• 1954–70; 1898-1955; 1971–present: This version started the story when Mrs. Clark met Rosa Parks, someone familiar to readers.

• 1947–70; 1898–46; 1971–present: This version — the one I finally chose — started the story at the end of World War II, when Mrs. Clark returned to Charleston. It seemed more satisfactory than any other sequence because it focused squarely on the civil rights movement, which began, I came to believe, with the return of black soldiers from their military service in Europe and Africa. One of the milestones in the civil rights movement proved to be Judge Waring's decision that permitted blacks to vote in South Carolina's primary election. Since knowing the Warings really got Mrs. Clark's life moving, this became an effective place to start her story — the personally and publicly significant moment coincided.

Fortunately, once you have written your narrator's story in one sequence, it is relatively easy to try others. Just xerox two copies and save one to start all over from in case you don't like what you try first. Play around with the sequence by cutting and pasting until you find the best solution.

Whose Book Is It?

By the time you have put in as much work as it takes to produce a finished, lengthy manuscript, you are going to be thinking of this as your book. Let's face it, who really wrote it anyway? Your narrator just talked about it.

When you make a careful analysis, you have to admit that the book belongs to both of you, a genuine collaboration. It would not exist without the work of both of you. The experience, the words, the story are your narrator's, but you had the skill to put them on paper and shape them into a readable form.

You realize now, if you did not at the outset, that writing someone's oral biography is helping that person write his or her autobiography. How is authorship attributed on books like this, when it consists of a subtle, back and forth collaboration?

There is a variety of ways that authorship is indicated on oral biographies. *Ready from Within: Septima Clark and the Civil Rights Movement* is handled in an unusual way. It puts Mrs. Clark's name in the title, identifies the book as a first-person narrative in a sub-title, and adds that Cynthia Stokes Brown edited the text. A more common way to attribute authorship of an oral history is to state that the book is "by" the narrator "with" the editor, as in *Let Me Speak!: Testimony of Domitila, a Woman of the Bolivian Mines* by Domitila Barrios de Chungara with Moema Viezzer. Sometimes an oral biography is attributed to the narrator "as told to" the transcriber/writer. This form is usually used for celebrities who hire someone to write their story, as in: Henry Fonda, *Fonda: My Life*, as told to Howard Teichmann. The form "edited by" is usually reserved for accounts that have been written as memoirs by their narrator and edited by someone else to prepare them for publication; for example: *The Montgomery Bus Boycott and the Women Who Started It: the Memoir of JoAnn Gibson Robinson*, edited, with a foreword, by David J. Garrow. Sometimes full authorship is attributed to the oral historian; in the following case it was done because the narrator might have been in danger if his real name were known: Theodore Rosengarten, *All God's Dangers: The Life of Nate Shaw*.

CHAPTER 8

Writing from Multiple Narratives

Suppose you want to talk to various people about some topic—the civil rights movement, the Vietnam War, the history of your town, or recent immigration to your city. How would you go about structuring a piece out of a series of different narratives?

Some Examples

Since my book *Ready from Within* cannot serve as a model for that, look around for some that can. For example, look at Studs Terkel's wonderful oral histories, many of them best sellers (see the list of them in the Resources section). Terkel's books are more journalistic than historical. What he does best is to stir people to talk about their real feelings with honesty and candor.

To organize his book about the Great Depression, Terkel divided it into five sections, or books, each untitled. Each book contains several titled sections. For example, Book Two contains "Old Families," "Members of the Chorus," "High Life," "At the Clinic," "Sixteen Ton," "The Farmer Is the Man," "Editor and Publisher." Book Six contains "The Fine and Lively Arts," "Public Servant," "The City," "Evictions, Arrests and Other Running Stories," "Honor and Humiliation," "Strive and Succeed." This all seems rather loose, built as it is on feelings and general connections, but it covers all the bases in a thorough and compelling way. In most of the titled sections named above, several different people speak. Terkel introduces each one briefly—usually giving name, age, and a comment: "A car dealer. He has a house in the suburbs." Sometimes this brief introduction consists of a quotation from the narrator: "I'm seventy-one and I can still swim."

Terkel usually lets his narrators talk uninterrupted. If they mention something that the reader may not be familiar with, he makes a footnote. Usually their narratives are quite short. If a narrative continues and shifts topics, then the question asked by Terkel is left in the text so that the reader can see how the shift takes place. If Terkel wants to add information, a comment of his own, or a comment by the narrator, he does.

Another fine book organized like Studs Terkel's is *My Soul Is Rested: Movement Days in the Deep South Remembered* by Howell Raines. He divides it into two parts; the first is subdivided into chapters with these topics: "The Beginning," "Black Surprise," "Freedom Rides," "Alabama," and "Mississippi." The second has chapters with accounts about "Down-Home Resistance," "Higher Education," "Lawyers and Lawmen," "Reporters," "Assorted Rebels," and "Black Camelot." Raines transcribed the words of the various people he interviewed and put on paper the authentic qualities of these people who made history.

A Sample Project

Suppose you are interested in how people in your town felt about the civil rights movement when they were young and how they feel about it now. You like the idea of writing from several different narratives in order to present different voices and points of view. How could you go about doing it?

Since conducting many interviews is a lot of work, you may want to do it with friends or classmates.

Once you have decided on a topic, or an area to explore, it's best to develop the main questions you want to ask, even before approaching your narrators. Reread chapter 3 on asking questions. The way you want to focus your story determines what questions you want to ask, and conversely, the questions that you ask produce the substance of your story. It pays off to plan ahead.

If you are working with friends, you can brainstorm this part together. Have one person copy down the questions on a big piece of paper or on a blackboard, where all of you can see all the questions you can think of.

After you've made this list, go back and consider each one: whether to keep it or eliminate it, how to improve it, where it should go in the sequence of questions.

Here are questions that could be asked about the civil rights movement. This general list wouldn't work well until it's tailored to fit a particular town; it would be much different for Berkeley, California, than for Montgomery, Alabama.

- How did the civil rights movement affect your town?
- What was it like for you during the movement?
- How did you learn about what was going on during the movement?
- What do you know about Rosa Parks? How did you learn about her? How do you feel about what she did?
- What did you think about Martin Luther King, Jr.?
- Do you think that black people should have used violence to achieve their goals?
- What did you think about the Supreme Court decision in 1954 that said separate schools for blacks was unconstitutional? When were schools integrated in your town? What was your experience during that?
- How did you feel about the sit-ins? If you had been in the South, would you have participated?
- Did you have any black/white friends then? Now?
- What role did your church play in the civil rights movement? In your thinking about it?
- Do you feel that black people are better off today than they were in the fifties? All over the country? In this town? What do you think is going to happen to black people in the future?
- Do you think that teachers should teach about the civil rights movement in schools today? What do you want your grandchildren to learn about it?
- Did you have any civil rights issue here in this city? How were they resolved? Do you have any now? How are you involved?

If you have trouble thinking of questions to ask, then probably you don't know enough about your topic. If you have read *Ready from Within*, you probably have enough background about the civil rights movement. But on some other historical topic, you might need to read more about it to help you generate questions.

Once you have a good group of questions, you're ready to find some possible narrators. Talk together about what your town is like and who in it is likely to remember the civil rights movement. Remember, the dramatic events started about 1954. People who remember them were probably at least fifteen years old at the time, so

84

they would be at least forty-six or so now. If you restrict your narrators to those who actually remember, then you will be looking for people forty-six and over.

If you are in a large city not in the South, you can probably find enough people who left the South during or after the movement days. Even if you are in a small city, think about this category. You might be surprised at how many ex-Southerners live in your town. How can you find them? Try the grapevine. Ask around and see if anyone knows just one. As soon as you find one, he will know some others. (Here in the San Francisco Bay area, all the people who used to live in my hometown, Madisonville, Kentucky, gather occasionally for dinner. There are about ten of us.)

If you are not in the South, maybe you will want to focus your study on what people *not* in the South felt about what was going on there.

Will you want to interview white people or black people or both? How about Asians and Hispanics and native Americans? Should you limit your study to those who lived through the civil rights movement—or should your focus be on what the next generation feels, or on what your generation feels?

There are many decisions to make about whom to approach for an interview. Once you have identified potential narrators, your next step is to contact them. What should you say?

Call them up and be straightforward by explaining who you are and what your intentions and goals are.

> I am Julia, Tom Snyder's daughter and a student at the community college. I am very interested in the history of the civil rights movement and want to find out how it affected our community. I've been told that you have lived here since the fifties. Is that correct? Would you be willing for me to come and talk with you about your experiences during the days of the civil rights movement? I would like to tape record our interview because I may want to write an article about this. I plan to interview other people, too. I will be sure that you receive a copy of my transcription of the tape, and I won't use anything without your permission. When would it be convenient for me to meet you? I would like to spend about forty-five minutes with you.

That is what needs to be said, in any order and a lot slower. If you meet with resistance or reluctance, you might ask if you could meet with them to explain more about what you want to do before you start. Remember that it is harder for someone to say no in person than on the telephone.

85

Next you will conduct the interviews and transcribe the tapes. See chapters 2, 3, and 4 for reminders about these steps.

This is a more complex assignment than interviewing one person several times. You will need to introduce to your readers each of the people you interview. Be sure to get on tape, preferably right at the beginning, the basic information about your narrator. Ask them to begin by telling a little about themselves.

When you finish the transcriptions, you're ready to create a structure and begin writing. With this much material, it is more difficult to figure out what the richest and most interesting areas are. Making piles on the table and labeling the categories (as described under "Sequence" in chapter 5) will help.

When you cut the second copy of your transcript into pieces, remember to put the name of the narrator on each piece so that you can identify the speaker. Devise a name for each category that the material seems to fall into. Here are some categories that come out of the sample questions above.

• Rosa Parks
• Martin Luther King, Jr.
• School integration
• Role of churches
• Violence vs. non-violence
• How blacks felt about whites
• How whites felt about blacks
• The future for blacks
• The results of the civil rights movement

But your questions may have been different, and all kinds of material may have emerged that you didn't expect during the interviews.

Once your material is sorted, you can decide which topics to use and which to omit. Make a file folder of material on each topic that you decide to use. Each file folder can eventually become a chapter. You need to find a good sequence for the different narrators. You need to write an introduction to each chapter and to each narrator, and to add footnotes to give the readers background about places and events they might not be familiar with.

If you are working in a group, this work can be shared by dividing the folders (chapters) equally among you. If you prefer to work in pairs on each chapter, do that.

Once you have assembled each chapter, you have a first draft of your book. Work out a way to organize all the chapters and write a table of contents.

Now the job of editing begins. Review the overall structure and balance. Is there anything that should be left out—or restored? Does the sequence make sense? Now that you see the whole picture, what is a good title? Several drafts may follow as you review the structure and each chapter, down finally to the spelling and punctuation. Remember, if you are working in teams and groups, you can edit for each other and perhaps improve the manuscript faster than if you work alone.

Finally, you have only to figure out how to present your work, by reading it aloud or by xeroxing copies. Congratulations! You have worked through a highly complex task to its conclusion.

Here is a summary of the steps you have learned, with increasing ease, to take:

1. Decide the topic.
2. If needed, read background material.
3. List questions to ask.
4. Identify possible narrators.
5. Contact them.
6. Conduct interviews.
7. Transcribe interviews.
8. Check transcriptions with narrators.
9. Sort transcriptions into categories.
10. Research additional information.
11. Write introductions, transitions, and notes.
12. Edit.
13. Present the work.

CHAPTER 9

How to Do Oral History in the Classroom

For the purposes of this chapter I am imagining your class to be in senior high school social studies, but my suggestions can easily be adapted to junior high and college classrooms. They can also be adapted for history, English, and writing classes.

My suggestions differ somewhat from the way *Foxfire* ideas have been used in classrooms to produce oral history. The main difference is that *Foxfire* projects usually have been done in an elective class in English. I am suggesting that this kind of work be done in social studies or history class, that is, as writing across the curriculum. Therefore, in my plan the oral history work should not become the whole curriculum, as might be appropriate for an elective English class. In social studies or history classes, it needs to be kept small-scale, part of the mainstream curriculum, a way to deepen and enliven the customary course, not substitute for it.

So here you are, convinced of the value and excitement of writing from oral history and wanting to do it in school. If you are a student, this means persuading your teachers to try some of your ideas. If you are a teacher, this means figuring out effective ways to do it with the whole class.

But, of course, the whole process cannot easily be rushed into the whole class right away. Why not start slowly and naturally, simply by using current activities that lend themselves to developing the preliminary skills for writing from oral history?

Interviewing a Guest

For instance, you probably already invite occasional guests to talk with your class about some topic they know first-hand. (If you can't get a guest, *you* be the guest.) Let this be an occasion for your students to practice the skills of interviewing and writing from interviews.

Before the next guest arrives, tell your students what the topic will be and what the qualifications of the guest are to discuss it. Appoint a panel of two to four students to be the interviewers. Appoint a committee of two or three to operate the tape recorder; or have several committees of two or three to operate the tape recorder, or have several committees with several recorders. Select someone to introduce the guest. Other students can fill these roles for the next guest.

Have the entire class generate a list of questions for the interviewing panel to put to the guest. List the questions on the board and evaluate them. Eliminate ones that seem less likely to generate interesting answers; figure out a sequence for them.

When the guest arrives, the committees carry out their roles while the rest of the class listens, perhaps joining at the end with more questions that have occurred to them during the interview. During the next class period, play back the tape for the class to evaluate. Which questions worked best? Why? What questions might have been better? What portions of the tape are most interesting? What portions might one want to transcribe? Why?

After listening to the tape, have everyone write a short report about the speaker's visit. This can be done in class or at home. At the same time, appoint a committee of two or three students to transcribe and type short portions of the tape, but not so much as to be tiring. Distribute copies of these short selections to the class and have them revise the first drafts of their articles by working into them these exact quotations from the speaker.

Voilà! Your students have now completed their first oral history interview with a minimum of frustration and a maximum of cooperation. Discuss with them what they enjoyed and what they did not, what the problems were and what to do differently next time.

From your point of view as teacher, this method of interviewing the speaker takes more time than does the customary method (having a speaker and questions, all in one class period, with no preparation or follow-up). You will see whether you become convinced that the value of this method compensates for the extra time it requires.

Other Interviews

You can think of other simple ways for your students to practice these preliminary skills. Students can practice interviewing — the key skill — with each other in pairs. Suggest topics such as parents' work, favorite music, games played as a child, favorite trip, what religion means to them, how AIDS affects them, their parents' (or grandparents') values. Ask your students to take turns interviewing and being interviewed; ask them to discuss afterwards, with each other and with the whole class, how they felt in each role, what was difficult, what questions seemed to work best. These interviews need not be recorded or transcribed; they are practice in becoming fluent with interviewing.

Select a committee to interview the principal, the librarian, the custodian, or some other favorite or influential person at school. Select another committee to record the interview. Choose a historical topic, such as "What was school like when you were young?" or "How do you feel about your ethnic roots?"

Ask the class to help generate the questions that the interviewers will pose and, after listening to the recording, to analyze the interview. Do this several times, and soon everyone in class will have served on the tape recording committee and will be familiar with operating tape recorders. If any part of these interviews seems worth transcribing, encourage students to go ahead. Maybe they can make an interesting piece out of it for the school newspaper.

So far, perhaps you have been setting up activities based on the availability of just one tape recorder—yours. To expand your activities, you need to know how many of your students have tape recorders at home. Maybe everyone in your class has access to a tape recorder and you need make no provisions. But maybe only half do; then you can ask them to pair off accordingly.

If very few of your students have access to tape recorders, you need to find a way to provide them. Can you pick some up at garage sales? Can you appeal to the community for ones no longer in use? Appeal to the PTA or the school's supply budget for a cash grant? A set of five or six will suffice; then your students can work as committees, a good idea anyway. At about $15 each for a new one, the cost of six comes to $90, not an impossible sum. Maybe the school library (or media center) could purchase a set to loan to classrooms. Some solution will emerge from your own situation.

One of the most important goals of any project in oral history is for students to learn the values and traditions of their families, to feel connected with those values as they make life choices, and to see where those values fit in among the diverse values around the world. Interviewing their families becomes one of the richest and most significant sources that students can tap for their oral history projects.

A Sample Project

Many of the examples in this book have shown ways to interview family members. Here is one final topic that may prove captivating in classrooms.

Let the topic be "Your Family and War." Ask students to find out everything they can about their relatives' participation in fighting wars.

1. Finding People to Interview

Ask students to be family detectives and to find out what wars some members of their families lived through. Start with fathers or guardians, then ask uncles and grandfathers. Ask if there are family papers that might give information about further back, or people who know the family history. Have students explain that this is a preliminary investigation; now they are locating people to interview and soon they will be back for in-depth interviews. For this step, students can keep written notes; recording on tape will come later.

Point out that women are also deeply involved in wars, even if they are not combatants. Remind students to look for information from women — mothers, sisters, aunts, and grandmothers whose lives were changed by war.

2. Planning Interviews

In class, have students share their findings. What wars have family members been in? List them all on the board. Which students have connections with which wars? List that information. Which students have found people to interview from more than one generation in their family, say, a father and a grandfather who fought in different wars?

Use this information to form working groups of four or five students. Organize a group around each of these topics that students have found narrators for: Vietnam War, Korean War, World War II, World War I, and any war across generations (this would include students who have narrators from more than one generation). If there are more than five students who have narrators on one topic, say the Vietnam War, set up as many groups as appropriate.

3. Planning the Questions

Make it clear that students should expect a wide range of opinion. Some men take pride in fighting, others do not, and it may vary from war to war. Have the whole class generate basic questions to ask. If students do not bring them up, suggest these: Did you volunteer or were you drafted? How did you feel about going? What happened while you were in the armed forces? What happened when you came home? How do you feel about it now? What effect did your being away have on the women in your family? How do your feelings about war compare to your brother's? Your father's? Your son's?

Some sample questions to ask women are: How did you feel about this war? How did it affect your life? What effect did it have on your relationship to your sweetheart/husband/son/father? What did you learn from this experience? How did it influence your present feelings about war? What moment from it do you remember best?

4. Conducting the First Interview

Teach students the information they need to record at the beginning of the tape (see "Setting Out" in chapter 2). Ask them to tape an interview with their narrators, using the questions generated in class and any others that occur to them at the time.

5. Doing Research

Ask students to discuss what they've learned from the first interview. They might play parts of their tapes for each other, if there's time. Ask them to list topics that came up that they didn't understand completely. Give them a class period to research these topics in the library or in class. Ask them to generate another list of questions, more specific this time, to ask their narrators. For example: Why were twenty-six per cent of all casualties in the Vietnam War black when only ten percent of the population was black?

6. Conducting the Second Interview

Ask students to tape record another short interview with each of their narrators to clear up any confusing points and to get deeper into the material and the feelings.

7. Writing Up the Results

Ask each student to write an article based on listening to their interviews. After they have written a first draft, ask them to listen again and pick out a few passages that would make effecive direct quotations to add to their articles. Have them transcribe these pasages. For advice on transcribing, see chapter 4.

Students could then turn in their articles, or they could present them to each other in their groups and rewrite them again in light of their classmates' responses. Each group could produce a booklet on its war or on the different ways that generations view war. Each group could plan a class presentation based on combining the articles of each of its members in some way—talks and readings by each member, or making a new tape recording of students reading from their articles plus quotations from their narrators in their own voices from the original tapes. All this would take lots of time, but you would cover lots of material and students would learn lots of history and skills.

As you can see, these simple projects have a way of mushrooming, because often nobody wants to quit. The work becomes too interesting and provocative to let go of — a happy problem.

•

One tenth-grade student, Jennifer Kaufman, told me about doing an oral history assignment for history class in the eighth grade. Prior to this, she had had one experience with tape recording; in the sixth grade, she had taped an interview with a friend of her mother's. For this new assignment, Jennifer interviewed a family acquaintance who had been in Japan when the United States dropped the first atomic bombs on Hiroshima and Nagasaki. She had these reactions:

> Some kids think they are getting off easy to do an oral history instead of reading a book, but they found out it is much harder to get it out of a person than from a book.
>
> Interviewing is the closest you'll get to history. It is neat to be close to a person who has been there, telling you their experiences. It

93

is important that you are taking his life story and putting it on paper so that other people can read it. You're making what happened to him come back to life again. . . . Now, when I read history that I've been through, it's neat. I have a sense that I'm making history.

The questions were really boring; they were not personal enough toward the person. His account came out jumbled. I had to work through that and figure out what he was trying to say, then put it in my own words. I didn't get everything out of him the first time. I was rushed and wanted to call back; I didn't know what I was looking for.

I put the recorder too near the man I was interviewing, so it didn't record the questions very well. [It had a built-in microphone.] I learned that we both have to stay near the recorder. I also learned not to play know-it-all, but to play dumb and confused. I nodded when I understood, and I stopped nodding to make sure he knew when I was confused. Then he would stop to explain. I also learned not to cut him off, but to let him finish. It will intimidate them on the next question if you jump in too soon.

Other Short Assignments

There are many short assignments in writing oral history that you can work into your curriculum.

• **Grandmother/Grandfather Stories**

Have students ask their grandparents to tell them stories about their childhoods. If visits are not practical, this can be done by telephone or by letter. Students can first retell these stories and later write them up. This is a good chance for students to write language as it is spoken, not as standard written English. Students can bring in photos, mementos, and artifacts. Family time lines can be compared to regional or national time lines. A culminating "tea party" can be arranged so that all the students can meet the local grandparents. This assignment could focus solely on "grandmother" stories and could culminate in a women's history day during March, Women's History Month. For a resource catalog about women in history, write The Women's History Project, P.O. Box 3716, Santa Rosa, CA 95402.

• **"Then and Now" Essays**

Have students write "then and now" essays in which they describe current customs that they know well, and then go on to explore how the same matters were handled in their parents' or grandparents' day. They could conduct interviews, taped or not, with family, friends, or community figures. Possible topics are: schooling, teachers, dating, courtship and marriage, long winter evenings, popular music, sports, the roles of men and women, birth and child-rearing practices, burial customs, ceremonies, celebrations, food preparation, medicine and cures, religious and spiritual practices. Gender differences in the perception of customs should always be examined. In multicultural communities the comparisons can also focus on ethnic variations in the patterns studied, as well as differences between "then and now."

• **Biography**

Have students write a biography of a friend, sibling, parent, or teacher. For some period of time, maybe for two weeks, students would observe their person and keep a journal of these observations, including the results of one or more interviews. These journals could be shared and discussed in class. You could provide some categories for data-collecting and some interview questions; students could add their own. You could urge your students, when writing their essay, to bring their material into focus through one outstanding quality of their person or around one event in which their person revealed his qualities in action. Show, don't tell!

• **The Family Saga**

Have your students seen the television series based on Alex Haley's *Roots*, or read the book? Ask them to talk to the oldest member of their family and collect family stories that go back as many generations as possible. Students' grandparents may be able to recall something told them by their grandparents. In this project, students try to push back to the distant limits of their family's oral history.

To expand this, students could collect their findings and display them in a family history fair. Displays might include photographs, deeds, letters, artifacts, tapes and transcripts of oral history, and a map they make showing where and when their families have moved.

• **The Immigrant Experience**

Have students interview their families about the experience of moving and being a newcomer. Let them map the routes that family members have traveled; one can be considered an immigrant for having moved from one town or state to another. What was the route like back then? How did they travel? Why did they move? What attracted them to the new place? Remember that most of the ancestors of Afro-American students did not come to this country voluntarily, which makes their experience essentially different.

Contact local immigrant community organizations for groups of recent immigrants you might interview. Students in multi-ethnic classes may be able to work in pairs exploring each other's family experience with moving or immigration.

• Community Folklore

Folklore is the verbal folk art of a community. Some general categories are: fairy tales, ghost stories, tall tales, jokes, riddles, graffiti, songs, taunts, beliefs about dreams, superstitions, and raps. Children's folklore is a rich possibility: skip-rope rhymes, ball-bouncing rhymes, riddles, playground games, and taunts. Students could collect their own, those of younger siblings, and those of their parents and grandparents. Students can write these up from field notes or from tapes and create a booklet to present to the principal and librarian; the material could be used as the basis for a family night program or a school assembly.

• Chronicle of a Local Event

Students could study one significant event that happened in the community five to thirty years ago, perhaps a flood, a murder, a fire, the solution of a community problem (something positive?). They could interview eyewitnesses and consult primary accounts (newspaper accounts, diaries, letters, etc.). This exercise gives students practice in using primary sources, in seeing how different people have different perspectives on a given event, and in evaluating and synthesizing evidence to produce as accurate a narrative as possible.

• History of a Local Institution—the School

All students should study the history of the school they are attending, as well as compare schooling today with how it was for their parents and grandparents and how it is for children in other societies. Primary sources (people and documents) for school history exist right at your school. Generate questions with your students about what they would like to know about their school's past, and then help them figure out ways they can find the answers. There are many possibilities for interviews here. For more information, see Ronald E. Butchart's *Local Schools: Exploring Their History.*

- **Local Effects of National/International Events**

Another way to liven up history and give students a sense that they are in it is to direct them to study the local effects of some general topic in the textbook. Take, for example, the Great Depression. The textbook says that it was a period of hard times and social disorder. Let students verify whether that is an accurate description of what happened in their community in the years 1929-1939 by finding interviewees who remember.

Community Support

Short assignments like these give your students a chance to practice elementary skills and develop interest in oral history. These assignments also give you a chance to develop administrative and community support for this sort of study. In some communities, there are groups who believe that school assignments should not delve into personal or family information and should stick to the textbook. They believe that family experience and values are private and should not be examined at school. Because there is a diversity of opinion about this issue, it is important for you to inform parents and administration of your plans, goals, and rationale as fully as possible, even about short assignments in oral history.

As a good example, see figures 12 and 13 for two letters sent home by Beverly Ludwig, a second-grade teacher at Brookside School, San Anselmo, California. These went to parents before and during Ms. Ludwig's project on "Grandmother Stories" in March 1987.

Planning a Unit of Writing from Oral Interviews

After your students have practiced interviewing, you have tested your community's reaction, and you are sure of the value of this kind of work, then you are ready to embark on a longer assignment that will carry your students to higher levels of achievement. You might decide to undertake a whole unit based on writing from oral interviews, a unit that might take three to six weeks.

But how are you going to find three to six weeks within the required curriculum to teach oral history? What can you say to your department chair and to your principal to justify your departing

February 24

Dear Parents,

In honor of National Women's History Month (March) we are doing a social studies unit on women's history.

In culmination of this unit, the children will be assigned an oral presentation of a short childhood story from their grandmother's life (or mother, if there is no available grandmother). It can be from everyday life, school memory or some special memory of crisis, celebration, trip, etc.

If grandmother is nearby, will you help your child conduct an interview? Please write it down so your child can read it later to help prepare the oral presentation. If grandmother is far away, will you help your child write a letter requesting the information.

We will begin the "Grandmother Stories" March 16th. Please send a blank tape, so we can record your child's talk. We will also use this blank tape to record a sample of his/her reading. We also need a photograph.

I appreciate your involvement in our studies. This project relates to our "Family Tree" unit last fall and "Country of Origin." I'm enclosing a segment of a "Grandmother Story" published in "Faces" this month. We, too, will "publish" the children's stories. I value these portions of living history or "herstory." I believe children should be introduced to this value. Thank you.

Bev

Figure 12: Sample letter to parents

98

March 12

Dear Parents,

Today we began our Grandmothers' Stories. Several children were
ready to share the experiences. We are developing a bulletin board
titled "Herstory" with the figures of many famous women beginning
with the early goddesses. We would like to put pictures of the
grandmothers up on that bulletin board also;   THEY are certainly
famous women to our children and therefore a part of herstory.

Here is what we need -- AS SOON AS POSSIBLE

1. A grandmother story -- written down. Your child may
   read the story or tell it. Please have him/her practice
   at home.

2. A short tape for the tape recorder. (I have a few extra
   of my own for those that are unable to bring a tape)

3. A photograph or snapshot of Grandmother for us to put up
   on the wall.   It would be nice to have a picture of her as
   a child AND as a grandmother, but it doesn't matter that
   much. If you have no photo, that's all right, too.

At the end of the month, as a culmination celebration, we will have a
Grandmother's Tea -- the last week in March. I haven't
set a date yet. How does Friday afternoon, March 27th sound?

Yours,

Bev

We will share grandmothers
for children whose grandmothers
can't come.

Figure 13: Sample letter to parents

99

from the textbook in order to cover additional material? How can you feel confident that your students will be prepared for their standardized tests?

Since you plan to use only one unit's worth of time for this project, it can be considered an experimental unit that can hardly upset the balance of the whole year. Moreover, by careful planning you can fit it into the rest of your curriculum so that there is a logical and persuasive relationship to your overall scheme.

Here are a few suggestions. You can generate others by discussing the problem with your colleagues:

• Choose a topic that in the customary curriculum gets one chapter in the textbook—World War II, the Vietnam War, women's suffrage, slavery, the Westward Movement, or the civil rights movement. Substitute the oral history unit for the textbook chapter, or supplement the chapter with the oral history project. The further back in time the topic goes, the more difficult it becomes for the students to find narrators. Figure out what the students in your class might be interested in and what resources they might have. Involve them in the planning as soon as possible, even in choosing the topic. (See step 4 below.)

• Begin a year-long class in world history by using oral history to explore your community's connections to the world.

• End a course in U.S. history with a unit on students' family history that reviews all the major events of U.S. history by means of family connections to them. This may be pleasant to do in May and June when everyone wants relief from the textbook.

• Team up with a teacher in another discipline (an English teacher, if you're a social studies teacher, for instance). This will double your time, i.e., you can cover four weeks of work in two weeks because you will have a double period. This is easier to do in middle schools where there is sometimes a double period for the core curriculum of English/social studies. In high school it means you have to find out if any of your classes are scheduled all together for English, or if they all have the same teacher at different times. If so, you could plan a joint unit with another teacher for two periods a day, not necessarily successive ones.

• Use Black History Month (February) or Women's History Month (March) as your rationale for an oral history unit that explores the past of black people or women, or both and their connections.

Here are some steps you might take in planning such a unit:

1. Clarify Your Goals and Objectives

Your first job is to be clear about what you are trying to accomplish. What are your goals and objectives? State them clearly for yourself and then you will be able to explain them to parents, principals, colleagues, and students.

Only when you formulate your goals in your own words will you understand what your focus is and what you believe is most significant. However, here is a list of some possible unit goals that you can choose from, add to, and revise to help express your own special intentions and commitments.

• Students will become personally involved in studying history.

• Students will learn to think chronologically and across disciplinary boundaries.

• Students will acquire a deeper motivation for learning writing and history.

• Students from suppressed cultures, not well represented in the curriculum, will be able to insert their voices and their history.

• Students will examine family, community, and national values as these are revealed through personal history.

• Students will learn the skills necessary to conduct interviews and to write from oral accounts.

• Students will learn that preserving history requires effort and cooperation.

2. Inform Your Colleagues

You are prepared now to inform your colleagues and administrators of your intentions. Solicit their advice; listen to their cautions and work out ways to deal with potential problems. Find out who has had some experience in doing this, at other schools if not at yours. The more support and cooperation you can garner, the better off you will be. Explain to your colleagues that you have not yet worked out the details because you want to incorporate their advice and that of your students. Solicit the support of your school librarian and any school or community history clubs.

3. Motivate Your Students

To introduce this unit, you should think of something to grab the attention of your students and stimulate their energies for the work ahead. This might be something simple — you might tell a

101

"grandmother" story from your own grandmother. You might play a tape of someone being interviewed, a tape you made yourself or one you borrow from an oral history project. You might invite to class an elderly resident of your community who could delight your class with tales. You might ask your students to watch the "Oprah Winfrey Show" and analyze why she is an effective interviewer. You might show a short film about the Foxfire experience (see chapter 10 for resources). You might read "Septima's Childhood" from *Ready from Within* as an introduction to your students' finding out about what childhood was like in the past.

If you have time, you might begin by asking students to read some oral history — accounts from your own community, or some excerpts from Studs Terkel's books. High school students about to study the civil rights movement have enjoyed reading my introduction to *Ready from Within* as a bridge to understanding how it used to be. More advanced high school and college students might enjoy going all the way through *Ready from Within*, following the suggestions in chapter 1 of this book.

4. Plan with Your Students

Now that you have your students' attention, give them a chance to help plan the unit. Find out what they would like to learn through oral history, whom they would like to interview, what ideas they have about the topic. Ask them to talk to their parents and friends for additional ideas. Brainstorm the wildest possible paths to follow before you narrow down your plan. Revise the topic, if that seems desirable. Since your students' interests are key to the success of this work, spend enough time here at the beginning to engage those interests.

Another key to success is the parents' cooperation. High school teachers do not usually make the same effort to communicate with their students' parents as do teachers in the elementary grades. But parents are still eager to help when their children are teenagers, or should be, for their supervision is still crucial to students' success. This unit is the perfect opportunity for you to send parents a memo or letter describing the project and telling how they can help. Write a short letter, xerox copies, and leave space for students to add their own message. Or give students class time to compose a letter on the board that everyone will copy, ending with a personal message, to take home.

The final steps in designing a unit are more familiar and self-evident than these first four. Here they are in the proper sequence (they are discussed and illustrated in the sample unit plan below):

5. Organizing Committees
The work is divided up and students become clear about their responsibilities.

6. Practicing Methods
Students practice some basic skills of oral history.

7. Gathering Data
Students conduct interviews and verify their findings by research in the library.

8. Writing Up the Results
Students write summaries of what they have learned and integrate it into a finished document.

9. Communicating with Others
Students present their work orally, in writing, and on tape.

A Sample Unit Plan

Here is a sample unit plan for ninth-grade world history students. This plan takes into account the disadvantage of its being for the first unit of work, before you know your students and before they have time to practice any preliminary oral history skills.

OUR COMMUNITY'S PAST CONNECTIONS TO THE WORLD
AN INTRODUCTION TO WORLD HISTORY
1789–PRESENT

1. Goals and Objectives. This hypothetical unit is designed for classes in world history at Tamalpais High School in Mill Valley, California. This high school serves many students from affluent, professional white families. It also serves black students from neighboring Marin City, a working–class city of black families that came to load the Navy's ships during World War II. Tamalpais High School is currently 86% white, 7% Afro-American, 4% Asian, and 3% Hispanic and Philippino.

Given this situation, the goals for this unit are:

- Students will become actively involved in studying their community's history.
- Afro-American students, and other minority students, will feel involved in world history and see the role of their people in it.
- Students will become familiar with multiple perspectives on world events.
- Students will learn to conduct effective interviews.
- Students will learn the skills necessary to write from oral accounts.
- Students will create a chronological framework on which to continue their study of world history.

2. Informing Colleagues. At the outset I would describe my plans to my principal and to the members of my department. I would solicit the help of the school librarian and ask English teachers if they would want to be involved by assigning support readings in literature, or with movies or plays. I might even ask the art teachers whether they might have some complementary art projects in mind.

3. Motivating Students. To whip up interest in this project, I would try to locate an older resident of Marin County who could come to class and tell students about the large migration of black people who came to Marin City during World War II: where they came from, why they left, what life was like here when they arrived, what the war was about, and how they felt about working in it. I would ask the guest to let me do a model interview with him. I would ask a student to tape record the interview for future reference.

4. Planning with Students. After this introduction, I would brainstorm with students about everything we might learn during the next four weeks and how we might go about it. We would be exploring the connections of Marin County to the world, but not investigating them in great depth. Figure 14 shows what our brainstorm might look like.

After the brainstorming, I would ask students to compose a letter in class (I would write it on the board at their direction) to send to their parents or guardians describing the project and asking for their assistance. I would ask one student to copy it and give it to me to type and xerox a copy for each student to take home.

5. Organizing Committees. The schema of our brainstorming translates easily into seven committees, one for each of the ethnic/

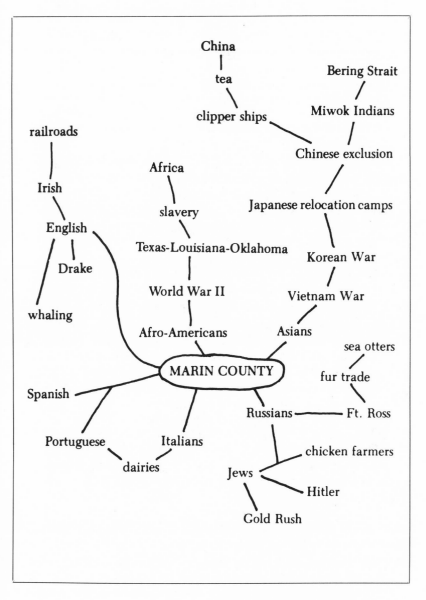

Figure 14: Sample brainstorm chart

national groups mentioned. For most classes, that would mean four or five students on each committee, just right. For smaller classes, I would combine some areas to reduce the needed committees to five or six.

Since this is an introductory unit, I would not know the students yet and could not predict their performance; hence, I might as well let them choose the committee of their preference. If they do, they are likely to choose their own ethnic group, if the class is diverse, and this is likely to work best. At this point I could not control the dynamics as much as I could later in the year; I would just trust the group process and view this as a getting-to-know-each-other unit.

I would review with my students how committees work and determine how much experience they have had with committee work. I would explain that every time they meet, committees need to assign roles to each member, rotating the roles frequently. Here are five roles that I would suggest they use: facilitator (who organizes and keeps the committee on task), recorder, checker (who checks that every member participates), research wizard, and supplies collector.

Next I would play the recording of the guest speaker and ask the students to analyze the questions—which ones elicited interesting answers and which ones didn't. Why and why not? I would teach them to distinguish between open-ended and closed questions. I would ask them to write up a brief summary of what the guest said. After they finished, I would hand out a few direct quotations that I had transcribed from the tape and ask them to work them into their summary. I would demonstrate how to transcribe from tape and let a few students practice.

To give students a sense of how much time I expected to devote to this unit, I would post the following outline. I could always lengthen it a bit if they became very involved and could not finish within this time frame. (Each number in the outline stands for a class period.)

OUR COMMUNITY'S PAST CONNECTIONS TO THE WORLD

Date:	Activities	Date:	Activities
_____	1. Guest speaker	_____	11. Gathering data
_____	2. Brainstorming	_____	12. Gathering data
_____	3. Organizing committees	_____	13. Writing and illustrating

106

_____ 4. Practicing methods	_____14. Writing and illustrating
_____ 5. Practicing methods	_____15. Compiling the booklet
_____ 6. Practicing methods	_____16. Compiling the booklet
_____ 7. Gathering data	_____17. Presentations
_____ 8. Gathering data	_____18. Presentations
_____ 9. Gathering data	_____19. Time line
_____10. Gathering data	_____20. Review (jigsaw lesson)

6. Gathering Data. I would explain that I expect students to use four sources of information for their work: 1) interviews with family and community elders, 2) interviews with leaders of local ethnic groups, 3) oral histories already existing on tape or in print, and 4) published local histories.

I would already have consulted with the librarian to locate 2, 3, and 4 above. I would either check out these materials and bring them to my classroom, or I would let one or two committees go each day to the library. I might need to bring into the school library materials from other libraries to keep on reserve for the duration of this unit. If the librarian agreed, students might invite some of their narrators to meet them in the library for interviews.

Students themselves would need to identify whom they wished to interview in category 1. Each committee could interview two people (one each in categories 1 and 2), plus whatever interviews the members of the committee could do on their own. Each interview has to be planned, conducted, taped, and outlined, with bits of transcription of quotable excerpts. The six class periods allotted in my outline will be busy ones. Some work will need to be done outside class.

7. Writing Up the Results. Students can listen to their tapes again and write summaries of what's on them. If there are many interviews, they might take notes from each one, using a different sheet of paper for information on each topic. Then when they write it all up, they can go from topic to topic, rather than from interview to interview, and compose a smooth narrative in their own words. I would help them do this by giving out sheets of paper (for note-taking) with a heading like this:

Committee's topic: _____

Sub-topic: _____

Narrator: _____(or)Published Document: _____

Interviewed by: _____ Publication Date: _____

Date: _____ Page Numbers:_____

If there were not enough time, or students were not yet skilled enough to integrate all their sources, they could string along a series of narratives that describe each narrator and what they learned from that narrator. I would encourage them to transcribe small parts of the interview to use as part of their narrative. I would also encourage them to include maps, drawings, charts, and anything else that might illuminate the text.

The final product would be a book about "Marin and the World in the Past," or some better title that the students would come up with. It would contain a chapter from each committee, typed or carefully handwritten.

8. Communicating the Results. For closure of a project like this, it is important for students to communicate their results to others. (See appendix A—for examples of culminating events.) For themselves, each committee can orally present its work to the rest of the class. The class can present its book to the library. If possible, make copies of the book for each narrator. If there's extra time, the class could create a radio show by taping their own narratives interspersed with excerpts in the voices of their narrators.

Review

For the final class review, I would create a class time line. (See chapter 1 for more discussion of time lines.) Each committee could agree on the most significant dates from its work to include on a class time line. Then one member from each committee could enter these dates on a line drawn in chalk on the board. This chalk line could be divided into sections; each committee would be assigned one section to draw up nicely on long sheets of drawer lining paper. Since this is a class in modern world history since 1789, the time line could run from 1750 to 2000, a total of 250 years. If space is available to stretch it across one wall, perhaps it can be fifteen feet long. Two hundred and fifty years divided by fifteen feet gives about sixteen years to a foot, or three-quarters of an inch to each year.

The line on each sheet would have to be entered at the same height from the bottom edge of the sheet. Each committee would enter the significant dates for its section, taken from the time line on the board, which contains the dates contributed by all the committees. When complete, this paper time line could be taped together around the walls of the class for the remainder of the year, as a reference for the rest of their study of world history.

A final class might consist of a "jigsaw" lesson. This is one in which students are grouped in two different ways — one group in which they learn something (the expert group) and another in which they teach it (the home group). The committees in which students have been working are the expert groups; they have already gathered and written their information. Today have the expert groups count off and have all the one's form Group 1, all the two's form Group 2, and so on. If there are seven expert groups of five each, then there will be five home groups of seven each. In these groups, have each student tell the others what he learned through this unit and what it meant to him.

Grading

Since this is an introductory unit with the purpose of involving students and creating a frame of reference, I would not give a written test at the end of this unit. I would ask committees to monitor the participation of each member; I would also monitor participation and would give individual and group grades for committee work. I would ask the students to write an essay at the end about what they learned from this unit. Testing for dates and significant events would come in succeeding units as we covered the textbook material.

CHAPTER 10
Resources

During the past twenty-five years, with the availability of portable tape recorders, writing from oral accounts has proliferated. Writers have been exploring every possible way to use oral accounts as sources for biography, history, politics, and fiction. The result is a fascinating profusion of literary forms, highly inventive and unconventional.

What follows are some outstanding resources, arranged by categories. These will provide captivating reading and good standards for the beginning writer of oral history.

Interviews

A good place to look for interviews of famous people is *Interview* magazine (19 E. 32 St., New York, NY 10016), started by Andy Warhol in 1967. Other magazines that feature a regular interview are *Playboy, Rolling Stone, People,* and *Paris Review.* Alex Haley, the author of *Roots,* created *Playboy's* monthly interview format with his interviews of jazz trumpeter Miles Davis and black leader Malcolm X.

Fallaci, Oriana. *Interview with History,* translated by John Shipley. Boston: Houghton Mifflin Co., 1976. *Rolling Stone* called Fallaci "the greatest political interviewer of modern times." She worked for the Italian newspaper, *L'Europeo.* This collection of her interviews with influential people of the mid-seventies exhibits her mastery as an interviewer.

Cultural Journalism
Massey, Ellen G. and Massey, Ruth E., eds. *Bittersweet Country.* New York: Doubleday, 1978. Written by students in Lebanon, Missouri.

Wigginton, Eliot, ed. *Foxfire 1-9*. New York: Doubleday, 1972–1986. These nine books were written by students in Rabun Gap, Georgia, who interviewed elders in their community to learn about the skills and values of earlier times.

Wood, Pamela, ed. *The Salt Box*. New York: Doubleday, 1977. Written by students in Kennebunk, Maine.

Biography

Brazeau, Peter. *Parts of a World: Wallace Stevens Remembered* New York: Random House, 1983; Berkeley: North Point, 1985. This excellent oral biography, based on interviews with friends, relatives, and colleagues, was written long after the death of its subject, the American poet Wallace Stevens.

Chungara, Domitila de. *Let Me Speak!*, translated by Victoria Ortiz. New York: Monthly Review Press, 1978. The story of a woman of the Bolivian Andes, wife of a tin miner, mother of seven children, and militant women's leader. Her story was written with the help of a Brazilian journalist and social anthropologist, Moema Viezzer.

Gillespie, Dizzy. *To Be or Not to Bop: Memoirs of Dizzy Gillespie*, with Al Frazer. New York: Doubleday, 1979. This is an especially interesting oral biography because it intersperses accounts by friends and family with those of jazz musician Dizzy Gillespie, achieving a kind of improvisational style and giving several perspectives simultaneously.

Rosengarten, Theodore. *All God's Dangers: the Life of Nate Shaw*. New York: Knopf, 1974; Avon, 1975. An oral biography of an 84-year-old black sharecropper in Alabama. Nate Shaw's real name was Ned Cobb. The story is based on sixty hours of interviews spread over sixteen sessions. This book, which won the National Book Award in 1975, doesn't need extra notes about the historical background because Cobb assesses his own story in the context of southern life.

X, Malcolm. *The Autobiography of Malcolm X*. New York: Ballantine, 1977. Alex Haley assisted Malcolm X in the taping and writing of this book, which was finished two weeks before Malcolm X was assassinated on February 21, 1965.

Fiction

Atwood, Margaret. *The Handmaid's Tale*. Boston: Houghton Mifflin Co., 1986. This is a science-fiction novel based on the supposed tape-recorded accounts found in the belongings of a woman who died under the tyranny of a society taken over by fundamentalist Christians, a theocracy in which certain groups of women are forced to be the childbearers.

Gaines, Ernest J. *The Autobiography of Miss Jane Pittman*. New York: Dial, 1971. This novel—in the guise of tape-recorded recollections of a 110-year-old black woman who lived from slavery to the civil rights movement—was made into a popular film starring Cicely Tyson.

Historical/Cultural Topics

Coles, Robert. *Children of Crisis*. Boston: Little, Brown and Co., 1964. A description, based on taped interviews and notes from interviews, of the lives of southern black children confronting the cruelty of segregation and struggling to overcome it.

Dunaway, David K. and Baum, Willa K., eds. *Oral History: an Interdisciplinary Anthology*. Nashville: American Association for State and Local History, 1984. An excellent introduction to the history of oral history, with contributions by Louis Starr, Barbara Tuchman, Allan Nevins, Alex Haley, Richard Dorson, and Eliot Wigginton. Haley's powerful essay describes how he did his work on *Roots*, including his return to the village of his ancestor, Kunta Kinte, in Gambia. Available from AASLH, 172 Second Ave. N., Suite 102, Nashville, TN 37201.

Fraser, Ronald, ed. *1968: a Student Generation in Revolt: an International Oral History*. New York: Pantheon, 1988. A comparative study of student movements in the capitalist nations of the North Atlantic rim, this exciting book is the first large-scale international oral history. Seven historians and two sociologists from five countries collaborated to collect the interviews and to write a political and social narrative that incorporates brief quotations from the interviews. This book shows how differently historians handle oral interviews than journalists do in constructing a book.

Gluck, Sherna. *From Parlor to Prison: Five American Suffragists Talk about Their Lives.* New York: Random House, 1976; Monthly Review Press, 1985. Oral interviews with five American suffragists, among the last of their generation still alive when these interviews were conducted in 1972-73. Newspaper accounts and the editor's introduction provide historical background for the narratives.

Hall, Jacquelyn Dowd; Leloudis, James; Korstad, Robert; Murphy, Mary; Jones, Lu Ann; and Daly, Christopher B. *Like a Family: the Making of a Southern Cotton Mill World.* Chapel Hill: University of North Carolina Press, 1987. "You don't have to be famous for your life to be history," says Nell Signion, one of the narrators in this book. The six authors interviewed 200 people who worked in the mills from 1890 through the 1930s.

Raines, Howell, ed. *My Soul Is Rested: Movement Days in the Deep South Remembered.* New York: G.P. Putnam's Sons, 1977. Interviews with mostly well-known civil rights leaders. It serves as a collection of primary materials that are not, in this book, interpreted or combined into a single narrative.

Terkel, Studs. *American Dreams: Lost and Found.* New York: Ballantine, 1981. *Division Street: America.* New York: Pantheon, 1982. *The Good War: an Oral History of World War II.* New York: Pantheon, 1984; Ballantine, 1985. *Hard Times: an Oral History of the Great Depression.* New York: Pantheon, 1984. *Working: People Talk about What They Do All Day and How They Feel about It.* New York: Pantheon, 1974; Ballantine, 1985. In these five books, Studs Terkel, the most popular oral historian, has written into history the voices of working-class and black people. Terkel, a Chicago radio talk show host, is a talented interviewer and journalist working in the documentary tradition. His *Immigrants: the American Dream* (two volumes) is available from Caedmon Records (a division of Harper & Row).

Terry, Wallace. *Bloods: an Oral History of the Vietnam War by Black Veterans.* New York: Random House, 1984. Finely crafted interviews resulted in these monologues that give a vivid idea of the senselessness of that war.

Resources for Students and Teachers

Allen, Barbara and Montell, Lynwood. *From Memory to History: Using Oral Sources in Local Historical Research*. Nashville: American Association for State and Local History, 1981. Both a descriptive guide to the oral materials available to local historians and a manual for evaluating and interpreting those materials. It will extend your ability to think critically about your materials and combine them in coherent narratives. Available from the AASLH, 172 Second Ave. N., Suite 102, Nashville, TN 37201.

Baum, Willa K. *Oral History for the Local Historical Society*. Nashville: American Association for State and Local History, 1982. *Transcribing and Editing Oral History*. Nashville: American Association for State and Local History, 1985. Willa Baum, head of the Regional Oral History Office of the Bancroft Library at the University of California-Berkeley, is known in professional circles as the "Dr. Spock of oral history." These two books, written for staff people in local history societies, provide professional information in a format and language accessible to everyone. Available from the AASLH, 172 Second Ave. N., Suite 102, Nashville, TN 37201.

Burchart, Ronald E. *Local Schools: Exploring Their History*. Nashville: American Association for State and Local History, 1984. This book is for adults who want to learn how to conduct local research in a professional manner. It offers many helpful ideas, especially on how to interpret photographs. Available from the AASLH, 172 Second Ave. N. Suite 102, Nashville, TN 37201.

Hoopes, James. *Oral History: an Introduction for Students*. Chapel Hill: University of North Carolina Press, 1979. This excellent text for college students shows how to use oral histories as part of traditional term papers in history classes and how to interview with historical rigor and sophistication. This book, with its chapters that distinguish personality from culture and from society, would provide advanced high school students with a fine introduction to what the historical imagination is all about.

Ives, Edward D. *The Tape-Recorded Interview: a Manual for Field Workers in Folklore and Oral History*. Knoxville: University of Tennessee Press, 1980. This more advanced manual is a bestseller among professional oral historians. Written in a vernacular style, it is a tough-minded presentation of standards of good work. Available from CUP Services, P.O. Box 250, Ithaca, NY 14851 (607/277-2211).

Weitzman, David. *My Backyard History Book*. Boston: Little, Brown and Co., 1975. Terrific suggestions for doing family maps, family trees, "Family Night at Grandma's," "History at the Cemetery," and much more, written for elementary students.

Wood, Pamela. *You and Aunt Arie: a Guide to Cultural Journalism*. Washington, DC: IDEAS, 1975. This 220-page, richly illustrated student guide was written by a teacher and her students in Kennebunk, Maine. It covers all the principal skills that students need for cultural journalism projects, such as setting the project in motion, making decisions, organizing a staff, interviewing, photographing, tape recording and transcribing, and involving the community. Available from IDEAS, Magnolia Star Route, Nederland, CO 80466 (303/443-8789).

Zimmerman, William. *How to Tape Instant Oral Biographies*. New York: Guarionex Press, 1981. This little book gives clear, simple instructions and is especially good for interviewing family members. Zimmerman gives excellent questions to ask. Available from Guarionex Press, 201 W. 77 St., New York, NY 10024.

The Foxfire Film (16 mm, color, 21 minutes). This award-winning film introduces teachers, students, and their community to the way *Foxfire* started, grew, and was adapted to other communities. Most of the narration is by students participating in the process. *The Foxfire Film* was produced by IDEAS and Audio Visual Productions and is distributed by CRM Films, 2233 Faraday, Carlsbad, CA 92008 (800/421-0833).

Resources for Teachers

Mehaffy, George L.; Sitton, Thadi; and Davis, Jr., O.L. *Oral History in the Classroom*. Washington, DC: National Council for the Social Studies, 1979. This is just a seven-page insert for a looseleaf binder, but it is surprisingly complete. You could launch projects in oral history just from this. Available from NCSS Publications, 3501 Newark St. NW, P.O. Box P, Washington, DC 20016 (202/966-7840).

Wigginton, Eliot. *Moments: the Foxfire Experience*. Washington, DC: IDEAS, 1975. This book presents the philosophy and learning theory that underlie Foxfire programs. Written for teachers, *Moments* describes four levels of student development. The first level focuses on confidence-building through basic skills; the second on application of these skills in supportive involvement with other students; the third on sensitive awareness of others; the fourth on creative independence within a community framework. Wigginton emphasizes using a *Foxfire*-type publication as a learning vehicle, rather than as an end in itself. Available from IDEAS, Magnolia Star Route, Nederland, CO 80466 (303/433-8789).

San Diego/Tijuana International History Fair: a Projects Manual (n.d., n.p.). This 63-page xeroxed manual was developed to guide students who want to enter the history fair. It's a model for the kind of guidance that teachers can give students doing historical research. This one, of course, is filled with details of San Diego/Tijuana history, but it could serve as a model for creating one for your community. Available from International History Fair Office, Center for Latin American Studies, San Diego State University, San Diego, CA 92182 (619/265-5780).

Catalogs

AASLH Press Catalog, published quarterly. Write to Marketing Manager, American Association for State and Local History, 172 Second Ave. N., Suite 102, Nashville, TN 37201.

Women's History Resources. National Women's History Project, PO Box 3716, Santa Rosa, CA 95402.

Two Examples of Extended Oral History Projects

In late fall of 1953 and early 1954, a project involving oral history took place at Reed School in Tiburon (Marin County), California. For ten weeks, one eighth–grade class, under the direction of its teacher, Joyce Wilson, studied the history of their community. Since these were the days before the marketing of the tape recorder, the children took notes with pencils to retain what they learned from interviews. They also used newspaper clippings, books, and pamphlets, and mimeographed 2,300 copies of their narrative. The class of 1955 issued a second edition of 150 copies. In 1958 a typeset edition (1,000 copies) was published under the auspices of the Reed School District Parent-Teacher Club. In 1970 the Parent-Teacher Club published another edition in observance of the twentieth anniversary of the Reed Union School District.

After the project was completed, Joyce Wilson asked each member of the class to write a theme entitled "How This Book Was Written." Then, she later wrote, "the individual themes were literally cut apart, sentence by sentence, and some sample chapters put together. At least one sentence from every child was included. The class voted to use the version that you now will read." Here it is:

How This Book Was Written

After many months of interviews, research, and just running around the countryside, the eighth grade has been able to finish this book. Maybe you would like to know how all this began.

Our class started our "Tiburon project" as a slightly unusual language assignment. Sometime in early November, Miss Wilson announced that since we live in an interesting (though small) community, we should know something about it. We all agreed. We were to see if we could find some of the old publications about our area and interview a few of the people who have lived here a long time to see if we could get some information on the beginning of our community. (Our school itself was named for the father of Marin County pioneers, John Reed.) We were offered three prizes of Savings Bonds and Stamps by the Tiburon merchants and the *Pelican* for the best essays. Our teacher drilled us in the correct way to contact a possible source of information and how to interview a person. We doubt if anyone realized how far our project would go at the time we started.

What's behind this book? How was it written? Was it the work of the teacher, or of the class? We'd like to answer all these questions. First came the notes, taken by the members of the class. Everyone worked on these personal interviews. More than seventy-five people have been put into our worn-out notebooks by our weary pencil stubs. On many interviews people could not give us factual information but as we went deeper into the background of the area, people came to us with information. It was like a dream come true. Once the book was started, everyone wanted to help. And many early pictures and maps were found. Many students went to San Francisco, San Rafael, and Mill Valley. Many of us visited the county court house and county libraries.

Miss Wilson mimeographed sheets on which we copied our information: general topic, specific topic, date of information, researcher, date gathered, source of information (name, title of book or publication, etc.), and a summary of the information on that subject. We transcribed our notes onto these sheets and put them into the various folders: Reed; Reed Heirs; Tiburon Memories; Belvedere Memories; and others. When we started writing the book, we divided the sheets into chapter subjects so that students working on the chapter could use everyone's information. Besides interviews and newspaper clippings we used nearly a hundred books and pamphlets.

The trips and talks were exciting, but to write chapters one must sit down and write. The fun of interviewing and going to the city was over and now the hard work began. The room was put in order. Pictures went up. Chapters were under way.

The name of our book comes from the names of our community; Tiburon is Spanish for shark, and Belvedere comes from the Italian phrase meaning high point commanding a beautiful view.

The eighth graders who wrote this book have worked for long weeks and we all feel sincerely that the time was well spent. The time you take to read this may be small, but the times you read about were great indeed.

You will go more than 400 years into the past. You will see many men being born, making history, dying. Many interesting events will unfold before your eyes. And these events unfolded before our eyes, too. We've had a thrill in bringing this book to you. We've tightened a sail and strained on a pole to bring John Reed's ferry to the dock. We've seen an earthquake, a tidal wave, the herring runs, open air dances. And we've loved every minute of it. Gathering information and correlating it has been an adventure as we've tried to bring you a factual history of *Rancho Corte Madera del Presidio*.

In the thanking of people who have helped us, a large amount goes to the parents of our class. Through their cooperation our many excursions have been possible.

We must give the most appreciation to our teacher, Miss Wilson. Without her patience, guidance and care, this whole affair would not have been possible. And we hope you enjoy *Shark Point— High Point*—enjoy reading it and enjoy living it, as we did.

Eighth Grade, Reed School, Class of 1954

•

Another example comes from San Diego, California, and Tijuana, Mexico. It might serve to inspire other projects around the borders of the U.S., or anywhere that social studies teachers want to stimulate competition in social studies and humanities similar to that being generated by math and science fairs and contests.

The San Diego–Tijuana International History Fair is a community education program that was begun in 1983 by San Diego State University, the San Diego Historical Society, the Universidad Autónoma de Baja California, and the Universidad Nacional Autónoma de México. The project encourages junior and senior high school students to explore the history of individuals, families, neighborhoods, and communities in the greater San Diego–Tijuana region. The fair provides these students with an opportunity to meet and share what they have learned about the history of their communities.

San Diego and Tijuana form one of the world's few population centers that truly and literally contains "international sister cities." Since today's students need to realize that stereotypes will not serve to explain past events or to solve future problems, a primary goal of this project is to bring students together from both sides of the border to share their research and conclusions.

Here is the prospectus for the International History Fair. (For further information, contact the International History Fair Office, Center for Latin American Studies, San Diego State University, San Diego, CA 92182-0044.)

History Fair encourages students to study the history of their communities by developing research projects on such varied subjects as the role of a particular individual in the founding of the community, the historical experience of a given family or ethnic group, the development of a neighborhood, the varying fortunes of a local business or industry, and so forth. Their search for material may take them to the contents of a trunk in an attic, to the books and documents held by area libraries and archives, to the backfiles of a nearby business firm, the records of a civic organization, or interviews with a retired civic leader. Such research projects may not have any significant effect on our understanding of the past, or contribute to any scholarly body of historical research. But they are very meaningful to the individual students, and help immensely to develop in them a personal understanding of history and where they fit in the context of the larger community in which they live.

Students may pick any topic they wish to pursue as long as it concerns the greater San Diego–Tijuana region. The rules of the Fair permit students to investigate subjects that concern either San Diego or Tijuana as separate historical entities, as well as the common border culture and history that unite them. The rules also allow students from both sides of the border to collaborate on joint projects.

History Fair is held during a weekend in the spring of each year, with the site alternating between San Diego and Tijuana. The upcoming 1987 Fair, to be held in March, will be in Aztec Center on the campus of San Diego State University. Student projects entered in the Fair may be presented in any one of several different formats: research paper, table-top exhibit, dramatic performance, or audiovisual presentation. For each of these format categories there are separate divisions for junior and senior high school students and for projects that are prepared by individuals or by groups of two or three students. All entries are evaluated by teams of volunteer judges, and the most meritorious are recognized with cash prizes that are distributed at an Awards Ceremony the week after the Fair. The Fair does not involve direct competition between San Diego and Tijuana students. Instead, identical awards are given to the best entries from San Diego and Tijuana in each of the Fair's several prize categories.

There is little doubt that in the past four years the History Fair has established itself as a viable program that makes an important contribution to the educational opportunities of students in the greater San Diego–Tijuana region. In the inaugural Fair in 1983, a total of 1,690 students and 92 teachers were involved. In 1986 the numbers had grown to 2,430 students and 123 teachers. For the 1987 fair it is anticipated that at least 2,500 students will participate. (Significantly, the proportion of San Diego and Tijuana students participating in the Fair has held fairly steady at 52% and 48% respectively).

In addition to quantitative growth, there has been a qualitative change between the initial and later History Fairs. In the first year, for example, all student projects were accepted for exhibit in the Fair. Since then, because of the tremendous interest the Fair has generated over the years, it has become necessary to conduct advance screenings to determine which projects merit inclusion in the Fair. As the entry process has become more competitive, student work has become more sophisticated. At first, projects tended to be static and descriptive. In effect, they provided a "snapshot" of the way things were at a given point in time. Now student projects focus more on explaining the reasons for past events or on exploring their relevance to contemporary concerns.

Interview Examples

Here is an interview you can analyze. It was conducted by a high school student, Alison Muller, at the Open School in Stockton, California, in the spring of 1978. The interview was conducted as part of the cultural journalism class and was published as a xeroxed pamphlet called "Meet the People." Notice when Alison develops an answer by asking another question about it, or when she changes the subject entirely.

An Interview with Michael McShane
by Alison Muller

ALISON: Please state your name.

MICHAEL: Mike McShane.

ALISON: This morning we would like to go back into your background and talk to you about your family and yourself. What is your occupation?

MICHAEL: Professional fool! No, I am an actor.

ALISON: What is the very first memory that you have of yourself?

MICHAEL: God. . . the very first memory that I have of myself is one time I shot my father. When I was a kid I had a set of cowboy guns. I remember my father came home from work one day and as he came around the corner, I jumped out and. . . Bang! Bang! Bang! He fell over and I thought that he was dead. I thought that I had killed him. I was really upset and I started crying. Then he got up off the ground. That really flipped me out.

ALISON: What kind of realtionship did you have with your parents?

MICHAEL: A real bad one.

ALISON: Why?

MICHAEL: I was adopted. My parents always had the feeling that I didn't love them as a real son. They felt that I had my reservations about them. They went out of their way to force me into their mold. They did what they would have done if they had had a son of their own. You know, they would just take it for granted that the kid was growing up on his own and you guided him along the way. Let him pretty much take the route he wants to, except they felt that it was very important that you bring him up honest. It was important to them to raise a person who has the capacity to love. They tried to set me with certain ideals that I just couldn't understand or agree with. At the time, my mother had had a lot of surgery and she was taking a lot of dope. . . a lot of codeine. . . stuff like that. She would get really spaced out. She would start yelling at me for no reason at all. My father wasn't a weak man. It was just that he could never seem to express himself very forcefully. He never hit me. He never beat me or anything bad. You have to understand—we were from Kansas. When my parents adopted me, they were in their forties. They were not youthful people. My mother and father both came from very strict households. My mother grew up in a large household. There were like nine or ten kids in her family. She was used to the fact that you don't ever get what you want. You had hand–me–down clothes, hand–me–down this, hand–me–down that. . . . They were both depression people. They figured that any little thing was the best thing. Whereas, if I had been raised by my natural parents, I would have been raised in a more youthful atmosphere. They would have been more liberal and more modernized. All of the rest of my friends had parents that were young. My parents were old. They tried to inflict older attitudes on me. Then I would go out with my peers who had younger attitudes. I was always conflicting. I would come home and conflict with my parents. I didn't hate my parents. I wanted to understand them. I wanted to understand why they were asking me to be someone that I didn't want to be. My parents are very distrustful of other people. The one thing that they would always remind me was that people are dishonest and they will take you for everything that you have got. You know, there is a certain amount of truth to that in the world. That's people — we vary. I think that for every person like that, there is a person who has the capacity to be human. . . to love. So I was brought up not to trust anyone — except my parents. I couldn't agree with that because I felt that there had to be more than two people in the world that I could trust.

ALISON: When did you start to realize that?

MICHAEL: I think that I was about eight or nine. I was an only child so I was desperately looking for a "brother affect" from somebody. Somebody that I could really hang onto. Someone that was my same age. Someone who wanted to get rid of me but still let me know that he liked me. A big brother image that would always come to your rescue when the chips were down. I never had that from anyone my age. Somebody that was moderately like me. I was really searching as a kid.

ALISON: What type of hobbies did you have?

MICHAEL: I drew.

ALISON: What type of art were you interested in?

MICHAEL: I drew monsters.

ALISON: Why do you think that you drew monsters?

MICHAEL: I love monsters. I love dinosaurs. I love getting the crap scared out of me. I was really into Godzilla. We would go to a theater and watch monster movies. Almost every Sunday we would do this—it was a ritual. After the movie, we would go out for hamburgers and french fries. My friend always had cherry pie—I didn't because I was fat. We would always go see monster movies. We would sit in the balcony and heckle the movie. It was great. The older I became the more obscene the remarks were. I was into the monster movies. I was into the special effects of monster movies. I drew other things too. I always drew my own birthday cards, Christmas cards, Valentine cards, and stuff like that for my parents and friends. I don't buy too many cards. My mother always used to say that if you do it yourself and put your heart into it — the finished product is even nicer. I think that it is a good thing. I always thought that I would grow up to be an artist. I was never really into acting until later in my life. I still draw, I just don't do it as often.

ALISON: Michael, do you still live with your parents?

MICHAEL: No, my mother and father live in Kansas. I moved out of the house when I was eighteen. I joined the army. I stayed in the army until I was twenty-one. Now, I am twenty-two. The army sent me out to California. I was stationed at Sharpe Army Depot. I worked as an illustrator. I left the army and decided to stick around Stockton for a while.

ALISON: Now what are you doing?

MICHAEL: I work for the Stockton Art Troupe. I do plays around the community and do some work in the college theaters. I do it for the experience. When I work on plays during the day for the Art Troupe, it is more like my job. At night, when I work on plays for the Civic Theater or the college productions, I do it more as a hobby. It is more of a recreation time. I don't like working eight to five. I guess that I am not ready for eight to five. I don't like to punch out. I never liked structure. The looser it is, the better.

ALISON: What types of things have you learned from being away from home?

MICHAEL: I think that I have learned that you can't hurry people. You can't force yourself on anyone. I know that you have to be willing to take a second seat to anyone for a while in order to make them feel comfortable in a relationship. If a person is going to always be the foremost person in a group, that is just no good. I don't like the idea of being competitive. It is good to be competitive if you are trying to improve yourself, but it is not good if you are trying to prove yourself to a group of people. I learned that people are pretty much the same all the way around. They like to be secure. I learned not to think about what could have happened, or what should have happened. As far as my acting is concerned, I learned that you have to know yourself before you can be an actor. It takes a lot of self-evaluation to act and bring something across on stage. I learned that you cannot fool yourself. I know that you have to keep your own sense about you and your own soul about you. You have to be able to accept what is changing without causing too much conflict within yourself and other people. You have to try not to let those changes affect the people that you love.

ALISON: Now who do you depend on for a relationship?

MICHAEL: There is no one particular person that I get my strength from. I get my strength from all of my friends. I think that because I was an only child, I learned to get most of my strength from myself. You should be your own hardest critic. I get a great deal of strength from the people that I am surrounded by now. I am always trying to see if a relationship that I have with a certain person can be stronger. I am always trying to be helpful. I am willing to lay myself down for anyone that I know and love. Eventually, I expect the same from them, too. I guess that it isn't that I expect it but that I hope that it will happen. If it doesn't happen, I won't get all uptight.

ALISON: What type of backgrounds do your friends come from?

MICHAEL: Some are actors, some are just everyday people. One of my roommates is a stock boy, the other is a cook at Rare Steer. They

come from all sorts of backgrounds. My roommates are both basically ordinary people. They both have a lot of life. That is what I appreciate about them the most. They are both extremely sensitive. A
lot of my friends are pretty unsure where they are at—just like the
rest of us.

ALISON: What kind of advice can you give us?

MICHAEL: Don't kid yourself. Don't lie to yourself and think that it
will become a truth later on. Don't try to hurt other people. You
should take everyone at first with a grain of salt. Don't deny them.
Be your own best friend. You are going to find that when high
school ends, a lot of your relationships with people are going to end.

ALISON: What is the one unique thing about yourself?

MICHAEL: My imagination. No one can take that away from me.
That is the thing that keeps me alive. That is the thing that makes
my life full.

ALISON: Michael, thank you for coming and talking to us today. I
hope that we can do it again sometime.

MICHAEL: I would like that. Thank you.

From Oriana Fallaci's
Interview with the Shah of Iran

One master of the oral interview is Oriana Fallaci, an Italian
journalist. She interviewed famous people so skillfully that they
often revealed far more about themselves and their ideas than they
ever intended. Reading Fallaci's interviews is a good way to learn
how to frame challenging and provocative questions and to respond
sensitively. Here is a sample of how she did it; this is the beginning
of her interview with the late Shah of Iran, Mohammed Riza
Pahlavi, conducted in Teheran in October 1973 and published in
Interview with History (Houghton Mifflin, 1976).

ORIANA FALLACI: First of all, Majesty, I'd like to talk about yourself
and your position as king. There are so few kings left, and I can't get
out of my head something you said in another interview: "If I could
do it over again, I'd be a violinist, or a surgeon, or an archaeologist,
or a polo player. . . . Anything but a king."

MOHAMMED RIZA PAHLAVI: I don't remember having said those
words, but if I did, I was referring to the fact that a king's job is a
big headache. So it often happens that a king gets fed up with being
king. It happens to me too. But that doesn't mean I'd give it up—I

have too much belief in what I am and what I'm doing for that. You see. . . when you say there are so few kings left, you're implying a question to which I can only give one answer. When you don't have monarchy, you have anarchy or oligarchy or dictatorship. And always monarchy is the only possible way of governing Iran. If I've been able to do something, or rather a lot, for Iran, it's due to the small detail that I happen to be king. To get things done you need power, and to keep power you shouldn't have to ask permission or advice from anybody. You shouldn't have to discuss your decisions with anyone and. . . Naturally, I may have made mistakes too. I too am human. But I still believe I have a mission to carry out to the end, and I intend to carry it out to the end without giving up my throne. You can't foresee the future, of course, but I'm convinced the monarchy in Iran will last longer than your regimes. Or should I say that your regimes won't last and mine will?

O.F.: Majesty, how many times have they tried to kill you?

M.R.P.: Twice, officially. And then. . . God only knows. But what does it matter? I don't live with the obsession of being killed. Really. I never think about it. There was a time when I did. Fifteen years ago, for instance. I said to myself, Oh, why go to that place? What if they've planned to assassinate me and they kill me? Oh, why take that plane? What if they've planted a bomb and it goes off in flight? Not any more. Now the fear of dying is something I don't feel. And courage and defiance have nothing to do with it. Such equanimity comes from a kind of fatalism, from blind faith in the fact that nothing can happen to me until the day I've carried out my mission to the end. Yes, I'll stay alive until such time as I finish what I have to finish. And that day has been set by God, not by those who want to kill me.

O.F.: Then why are you so sad, Majesty? I may be wrong, but you always have such a sad and worried look.

M.R.P.: Maybe you're right. Maybe I'm a sad man at heart. But my sadness is a mystical one, I think. A sadness that comes from my mystical side. I wouldn't know how else to explain it, since there's no reason why I should be sad. I now have everything I wanted as a man and as a king. I really have everything, my life goes forward like a beautiful dream. Nobody in the world should be happier than I, and yet. . .

O.F.: And yet a cheerful smile on your part is rarer than a shooting star. Don't you ever laugh, Majesty?

M.R.P.: Only when something funny happens to me. But it has to be something really very funny. Which doesn't happen often. No, I'm not one of those people who laugh at everything silly, but you must understand that my life has always been so difficult, so exhausting. Just think of what I had to put up with during the first twelve years of my reign. Rome in 1953...Mossadegh...remember? And I'm not even referring to my personal sufferings—I'm referring to my sufferings as a king. Besides, I can't separate the man from the king. Before being a man, I'm a king. A king whose destiny is swayed by a mission to be accomplished. And the rest doesn't count.

o.f.: My goodness, it must be a great nuisance! I mean, it must be pretty lonely being a king instead of a man.

m.r.p.: I don't deny I'm lonely. Deeply so. A king, when he doesn't have to account to anyone for what he says and does, is inevitably very much alone. But I'm not entirely alone because I'm accompanied by a force that others can't see. My mystical force. And then I get messages. Religious messages. I'm very, very religious. I believe in God, and I've always said that if God didn't exist, it would be necessary to invent him. Oh, I feel so sorry for those poor souls who don't have God. You can't live without God. I've lived with God ever since the age of five. That is, since God gave me those visions.

o.f.: Visions, Majesty?

m.r.p.: Yes, visions. Apparitions.

o.f.: Of what? Of whom?

m.r.p.: Of prophets. Oh, I'm surprised you don't know about it. Everyone knows I've had visions. I even wrote it in my autobiography. As a child I had two visions. One when I was five and one when I was six. The first time, I saw our Prophet Ali, he who, according to our religion, disappeared to return on the day when he would save the world. I had an accident—I fell against a rock. And he saved me—he placed himself between me and the rock. I know because I saw him. And not in a dream—in reality. Material reality, if you see what I mean. I was the only one who saw him. The person who was with me didn't see him at all. But no one else was supposed to see him except me because...Oh, I'm afraid you don't understand me.

o.f.: Indeed I don't, Majesty. I don't understand you at all. We had got off to such a good start, and instead now...This business of visions, of apparitions...It's not clear to me, that's all.

m.r.p.: Because you don't believe. You don't believe in God, you don't believe me. Many people don't. Even my father didn't believe it. He never believed it, he always laughed about it. Anyway many people, albeit respectfully, ask if I didn't ever suspect it was a fantasy. My answer is no. No, because I believe in God, in the fact of having been chosen by God to accomplish a mission. My visions were miracles that saved the country. My reign has saved the country and it's saved it because God was beside me. I mean, it's not fair for me to take all the credit for myself for the great things that I've done for Iran. Mind you, I could. But I don't want to, because I know that there was someone else behind me. It was God. Do you see what I mean?

o.f.: No, Majesty. Because... well, did you have these visions only as a child, or have you also had them later as an adult?

m.r.p.: I told you, only as a child. Never as an adult—only dreams. At intervals of one or two years. Or even every seven or eight years. For instance, I once had two dreams in the span of fifteen years.

o.f.: What dreams, Majesty?

m.r.p.: Religious dreams. Based on my mysticism. Dreams in which I saw what would happen in two or three months, and that happened just that way in two or three months. But what these dreams were about, I can't tell you. They didn't have to do with me personally; they had to do with domestic problems of the country and so should be considered as state secrets. But perhaps·you'd understand better if instead of the word dreams I used the word presentiments. I believe in presentiments too. Some believe in reincarnation, I believe in presentiments. I have continuous presentiments, as strong as my instinct. Even the day when they shot at me from a distance of six feet, it was my instinct that saved me. Because, instinctively, while the assassin was emptying his revolver at me, I did what in boxing is called shadow dancing. And a fraction of a second before he aimed at my heart, I moved aside in such a way that the bullet went into my shoulder. A miracle. I also believe in miracles. When you think I've been wounded by a good five bullets, one in the face, one in the shoulder, one in the head, two in the body, and that the last one stuck in the barrel because the trigger jammed... You have to believe in miracles. I've had so many air disasters, and yet I've always come out unscathed—thanks to a miracle willed by God and the prophets. I see you're incredulous.

o.f.: More than incredulous, I'm confused. I'm confused, Majesty, because... Well, because I find myself talking to a person I hadn't foreseen. I knew nothing about these miracles, these visions... I came here to talk about oil, about Iran, about you.... Even about your marriages, your divorces.... Not to change the subject, but those divorces must have been quite dramatic. Weren't they, Majesty?

129

OTHER T&W PUBLICATIONS OF INTEREST

The Story in History: Writing Your Way into the American Experience by Margot Fortunato Galt. Practical exercises give students and teachers of all levels an entirely new way to view history—by reexperiencing it from the vantage point of the imaginative writer.

Personal Fiction Writing: A Guide for Writing from Real Life for Teachers, Students, & Writers by Meredith Sue Willis. "A terrific resource for the classroom teacher as well as the novice writer" —*Harvard Educational Review*.

Origins by Sandra R. Robinson with Lindsay McAuliffe. A new way to get students excited about language: the fascination of word origins. Includes many writing exercises and a brief history of English. "Refreshing and attractive" —Robert MacNeil.

The Teachers & Writers Handbook of Poetic Forms, edited by Ron Padgett. A clear, concise guide to 74 different poetic forms, their histories, examples, and how to use them. "A treasure" —*Kliatt*.

The Writing Workshop, Vols. 1 & 2 by Alan Ziegler. A perfect combination of theory, practice, and specific assignments. "Invaluable to the writing teacher" —*Contemporary Education*.

The Whole Word Catalogue, Vols. 1 & 2. T&W's best-selling guides to teaching imaginative writing. "*WWC 1* is probably the best practical guide for teachers who really want to stimulate their students to write" —*Learning*. "*WWC 2* is excellent. . . Makes available approaches to the teaching of writing not found in other programs" —*Language Arts*.

•

For a complete catalogue of T&W books, magazines, audiotapes, videotapes, and computer writing games, contact:
Teachers & Writers Collaborative
5 Union Square West
New York, NY 10003-3306
(212) 691-6590